Madame Wong's LONG-LIFE CHINESE COOKBOOK

S. T. Ting Wong with Sylvia Schulman

Illustrated by Linda Jarvis

CONTEMPORARY
BOOKS, INC.
CHICAGO

Published by Contemporary Books, Inc.
180 North Michigan Avenue, Chicago, Illinois 60601
Manufactured in the United States of America
Library of Congress Catalog Card Number: 77-92781
International Standard Book Number: 0-8092-7926-6 (cloth)
                                         0-8092-8030-2 (paper)

Published simultaneously in Canada by
Beaverbooks, Ltd.
150 Lesmill Road
Don Mills, Ontario M3B 2T5
Canada

This book is dedicated
to all of my students and friends
who have encouraged and inspired me
through the years.

Contents

Foreword

Our beloved teacher Mme. Wong is described in the Extension Bulletin of the University of California as:

S. T. Ting Wong, Formerly Teacher of Cooking,
Shanghai, Hong Kong and New York

This formal introduction in no way makes clear that what Extension students will meet in her classroom is a bombshell of intercultural energy who shares not only carefully treasured family recipes—mandarin and peasant, Cantonese and Shanghai—but her whole belief that foods are an integral part of any culture and must be known about, cooked, sampled and savored alongside a culture's technology, philosophy, literature and art, if one is to come to know that culture at all.

It is the nature of Chinese cookery (to which Mme. Wong attributes her long and healthy life) to be nutritionally sound. First, there is a natural *mixture* of various nutrients—fruits and vegetables. Second, there is no overcooking, which *saves* the nutrients. Third, there is a *balance* of nutrients within each menu—vegetables and proteins in the same dish. Fourth, there is a gastronomical *satisfaction,* an aesthetic extension of the nutritive values present.

Therefore, this is an unusual cookbook. Not only is it written by a cultivated "cook," but it is also written by a cultivated teacher—for her students, who are wild about her, and for others who will come, through her classes or this book, to know Mme. Wong's work and the beautiful spirit that animates it.

Robert Bartlett Haas, Director
Arts/Extension, UCLA

vii

Preface

Almost without fail, at the end of one of my series of classes, students come to me and ask why I haven't written a cookbook. Now, after forty years of teaching the art and science of preparing authentic Chinese cuisine, I feel impelled to put on paper not only the recipes I've most enjoyed but to share with you the specific skills and techniques that can open up a whole new world of cooking pleasure.

I grew up in a family that cherished learning. There are twenty-two doctors in my family. In China, we understand the correlation between eating the proper foods and maintaining health. We also have learned how to improvise, economize, and create tastes, textures, and aromas that have earned us a worldwide reputation for excellence.

By explaining the techniques of Chinese cookery, I hope to start you, as I have been privileged to start hundreds of others, on the path to a continuing education in Chinese cooking. The possibilities for variety are unlimited. The pleasure you will receive from being able to prepare a dinner in your own home that is better than any you could buy elsewhere and the fun of passing the skills along to your family and friends will make the effort you spend practicing the techniques more than worthwhile.

Madame Wong

Acknowledgments

The authors of this book wish to acknowledge with gratitude the invaluable assistance given by our typist, Peggy Jellison, our illustrator, Linda Jarvis, and our mentor, Howard Kaminsky. We would also like to thank Gail Reingold and Marjorie Thorsh for their assistance and Madame T. Z. Chaio for her help with the Chinese calligraphy.

A very special thanks to Samuel Schulman for his continuing help, patience, and understanding.

About the Authors

Madame S. T. Ting Wong

America's number-one teacher of Chinese cuisine is a dark-eyed, witty woman 72 years old. Born into a family of physicians who for generations had practiced in Shanghai, she carries her five-foot two-inch presence with that elegant charisma that marks a special person.

Presently Madame Wong teaches Chinese cooking at UCLA. She received a Western education at a missionary school in China. After her marriage she accompanied her husband to New York; she completed her culinary studies at Columbia University. She returned to Shanghai after the death of her husband in 1936 and founded the Shanghai Home Economics School. Soon Madame Wong had become internationally famous. The wives of English, American, German, and Japanese consuls were among her thousands of students.

After the fall of Nationalist China, Madame Wong was permitted to leave Shanghai to visit her ailing mother in Hong Kong. In 1956 she left Shanghai, never to return, and opened a cooking school in Hong Kong that was an instant success.

In 1961 Madame Wong returned to New York, where she conducted a series of special classes for chefs from famous restaurants, home economy experts, and writers of household magazines. Among her students were Albert Stockley, director-chef of the Four Seasons restaurant, and Elizabeth Gordon, food editor of *House Beautiful*. No wonder Madame Wong is called the teacher's teacher. In all, Madame Wong has taught more than 10,000 students, including many celebrities.

She has been teaching at UCLA since 1967. Her students love her and mother her. She is dignified, charming—a person who has overcome adversity and still maintains a great love of life, love for people, and love of teaching.

As you approach this book and learn the recipes you, too, will feel the buoyancy and excitement that Madame Wong's students have experienced from this ebullient woman. Her unique philosophical sayings are as important to her students as her recipes. We have therefore incorporated them into this book both for your pleasure and to give you insight into this consummate teacher.

Sylvia Schulman

Sylvia Schulman was born in New York City in 1920. She has been married to Samuel Schulman for 35 years. They have two daughters and two grandsons. She attended Goucher College and New York University, majoring in drama.

She is a braille transcriber certified by the Library of Congress, a vice-president of the International Student Center at UCLA, and recently has been appointed to the 11th district Medical Quality Review Board of Los Angeles County by Governor Brown.

Her hobbies are painting, tennis, needlepoint, and, of course, Chinese cooking.

Introduction

Shopping at a local market, I was amazed to see an elderly Chinese lady attempting to lift a case of canned goods. I rushed over to assist her, but she brushed me aside. She stubbornly insisted upon carrying this heavy box herself. I was so intrigued I followed her. By the time I reached her car, I learned that this 71-year-old dynamo taught Chinese cookery at UCLA. She explained to me how simple and healthful Chinese cooking is. She attributed her strength and longevity to her own style of cooking. She told me that if I followed her diet, I would be just as strong and healthy. After ten minutes of conversation, I enrolled in her class! Little did I know at that time how involved I would become.

The excitement of being a student of Madame Wong and the gastronomic joys I have given to my friends and family have encouraged me to prevail upon her to have her culinary secrets published.

I am confident this book will appeal not only to those who appreciate all fine foods but also to those who are health- and diet-conscious.

What is the secret of long life? I believe nutrition is the key. The recipes in this book are all highly nutritious. They are based upon those that have been in Madame Wong's family for more than 100 years. Madame Wong has the vigor of a 50-year-old woman. She attributes this to eating the proper foods. Many of us who have studied with her have changed our own eating habits. We are now her devoted followers and believers.

I know you will be ever grateful to Madame Wong for allowing you to enter the glorious world of her Chinese kitchen. Her recipes on the whole are not difficult to prepare; some are more intricate than others. But what is so rewarding is the great sense of creativity, serenity, and harmony that will permeate your dinner table.

This book is simple, direct, and easy to follow. Don't be afraid—plunge in! As Madame Wong says, "Only by doing it, you learning it!"

Sylvia Schulman

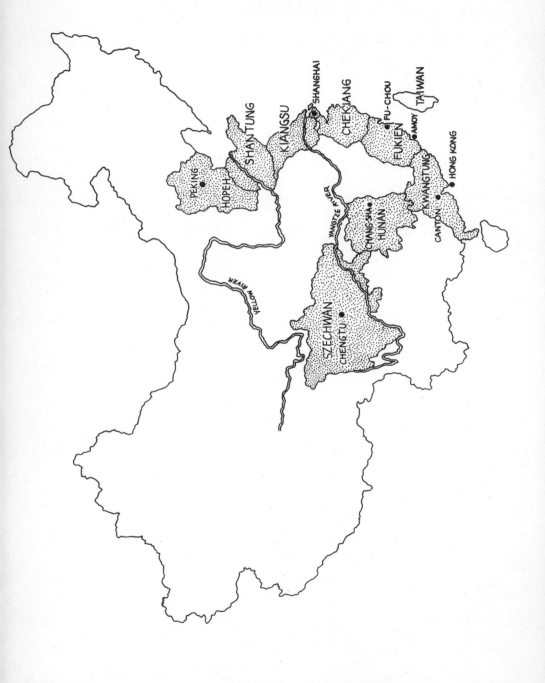

1

The Beginning

Food Characteristics of the Culinary Regions of China

SHANGHAI

1. More soy sauce and sugar than other provinces.
2. Unusual gravy dishes.
3. Wide range of seafood recipes.
4. Many varied noodle recipes.

PEKING (or Mandarin)

1. Wheat flour is staple food.
2. Many famous dishes served with pancakes and buns, such as Peking Duck and Moo Shu Pork.

CANTON

1. Colorful dishes: attention paid to appealing arrangements on serving platters.
2. Less soy sauce to retain natural color of foods.
3. Many fish and lobster recipes.

SZECHWAN

1. Hot, spicy recipes.
2. Salted meat and fish.
3. Generous use of garlic, red pepper, and leeks.

1

HUNAN

1. Hot, spicy recipes.
2. Many sweet and sour fish dishes.
3. Clear soups.
4. Many mushroom dishes.

FUKIEN

1. Best soy sauce in China produced here.
2. Many stewed dishes.
3. Clear and light soups.
4. Seafood often cooked with fermented red wine.

Equipment

A Chinese kitchen does not require many utensils. These are the few necessary ones:

1. **Wok.** The all-purpose cooking pan. You can improvise with a deep-sided frying pan, but a wok is more fun and cooks food more evenly and quickly. Before using, season your wok with oil and then place it over a high heat. Do this several times. Each time scour off excess oil that has burned. (Be patient.) This seals the pores and prevents food from sticking. You will know the wok is ready when the scoured bottom remains black. It is not necessary to use a strong detergent to clean your wok: a mild soap and brush will do the job.

2. **Steamer.** There are two kinds of steamers; one of bamboo that can be set right over the wok, and one of aluminum that is complete in itself. Both are used to steam or warm up food.

3. **Rack.** A rack should be placed under bowls or plates if you are using an ordinary pot for steaming. A tin can may be substituted if a rack is not available.

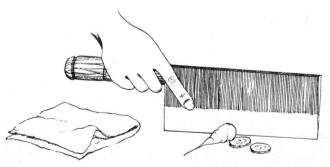

4. **Cleaver.** This broad, rectangular-shaped blade is used for cutting, chopping, shredding, slicing, mincing and transferring foods into bowls or pots.

5. **Metal Spatula.** A metal spatula is often used for stirring food to keep it from burning.

6. **Metal Ladle.** Food is scooped from the wok with a metal ladle.

7. **Cutting Board.** For chopping and slicing.

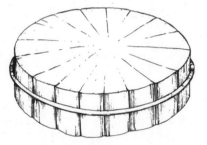

8. **Small Bowls.** After ingredients have been chopped, they are placed in small bowls. By having all ingredients ready, last-minute cooking is facilitated. Ordinary bowls can be used.

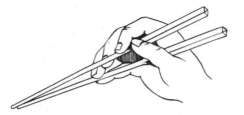

9. Chopsticks. Used for eating and also for stirring ingredients, beating eggs, folding dough, as in Basic Bun recipe—even for spinning sugar. They are sometimes made of plastic. Be sure to use wooden ones for cooking.

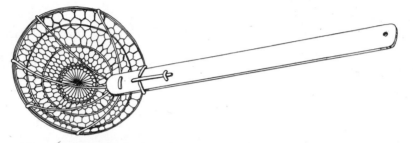

10. Large Strainer with a Bamboo Handle. This is used to remove excess oil from food when it is taken out of the wok.

11. Oil Strainer. A small strainer used to remove residue from oil.

12. Earthenware Pot. A heavy pot used for casseroles. Foods can be served directly from it.

Methods of Cooking

1. **Deep-Frying.** Heat two to four cups of oil to about 375 degrees. Place a small piece of scallion top in oil. When it turns brown, oil is ready. Drop food gently into the oil to avoid splashing. Food will change color when finished.

2. **Stir-Frying.** Use a small amount of oil and stir vigorously and quickly over high heat the entire cooking time, usually a few minutes at the most.

3. **Blanching.** Immerse vegetables (sometimes meat) in boiling water one or two minutes until color is heightened. Quickly rinse with cold water. This process keeps green vegetables green.

4. **Sautéing.** Cut food into small pieces and transfer to an open pan. Keep heat constant until food is tender.

5. **Braising.** Place food in small amount of liquid, cover pot tightly, and cook at low temperature in oven or over direct heat.

6. **Steaming.** Cook food covered on a rack over boiling water or in a Chinese steamer. Water level should be one-half to three-quarters full.

7. **Simmering.** Cook at low temperature (135-160 degrees) on top of stove. Bubbles appear and barely break.

8. **Stewing.** Cook in liquid deep enough to cover ingredients; liquid then can be used for sauce.

Care in preparation is essential. When you use a wok, always stir-fry small quantities. There should not be more than one pound of meat in the wok at any one time.

A Chinese chef, when using a cleaver, keeps a clean, damp cloth at hand and continually wipes the cleaver to keep the blade clean and sharp. As the story goes, when a chef is angry, he chops hard and the rhythm is heavy. When he is happy, the chopping sound is like music to the ear.

Cutting Techniques

The most important procedure in Chinese cooking is the way ingredients are cut and prepared. Therefore, you must provide yourself with a very, very sharp knife. A French cutting knife is perfect.

The Chinese are adept at using the cleaver, but this is a skill developed over the years. Any beginner is better advised to depend on his or her own trusty special knife.

In almost every recipe all the ingredients are cut to the same size and shape. There are three reasons for this symmetry: your food looks appealing, it is easier to cook if it is uniform and simpler to pick up with your chopsticks. (As you know, the Chinese do not use knives and forks.)

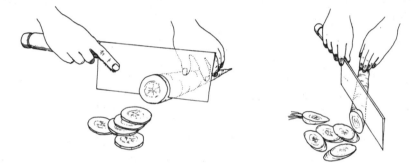

1. **Straight Cutting.** The knife is held straight up and down and the item is cut to desired thickness, from paper thin to ½-inch. Straight cutting is used for vegetables as well as meat.

2. **Diagonal Cutting.** The knife is held at an angle of 45 degrees for cutting. This method is used for any vegetable.

3. **Rolled or Oblique Cut.** The knife is held at an angle to the item while the opposite hand rolls the item, changing the angle while the knife cuts diagonally. Used primarily on carrots, eggplant, and zucchini.

4. **Cubing.** Ingredients are cut into small chunks about ½-inch square.

5. **Dicing.** Ingredients are cut into slices, then into strips, then into very small pieces about ¼- to ½- inch square.

6. **Mincing.** Ingredients are chopped into rice-size pieces—so fine that they almost become a paste.

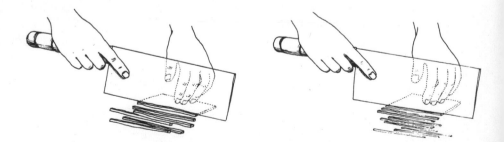

7. **Shredding.** Ingredients are sliced and then cut into thin strips.

8. **Julienne.** Ingredients are sliced and then cut into very thin strips that resemble matchsticks.

The Use of Oil in Chinese Cooking

One other secret of Chinese cooking is the use of oil. Any vegetable oil can be used; however, I prefer the polyunsaturated. To prepare the oil, heat the specified amount, add a slice of ginger and a sprig of scallion, and cook for about 5 minutes, until the ginger and scallion are almost burned to a crisp. Then discard them—they take away the raw smell of the oil.

This oil may be used over and over again for cooking meat, poultry, or vegetables, provided that ginger and scallion are heated with the oil every time to eliminate the smell of previous cooking. This deodorizing process always requires 3 to 5 minutes of cooking. Pour oil through your fine strainer to remove any residue.

For cooking sweet dishes or desserts, I always suggest that fresh oil be used.

Sesame Seed Oil is generally used as a seasoning. It is obtainable in Chinatowns or in many American markets or health-food stores. If you cannot find it, peanut oil may be substituted.

Pepper Oil is a very important part of seasoning in Szechwan food. It may be purchased in Chinese food stores, and a recipe is included in the Sauce section.

Helpful Hints

You will be more successful in your cooking if you read these hints carefully before you proceed.

1. Read entire recipe through before you begin to prepare the dish.

2. Most recipes are flexible. They serve from four to six persons. How much you will want to prepare depends on how many dishes you are serving—you must use your own judgment. If you find that you need more of any dish, double the entire recipe. Never add more chicken, meat, or fish to the seasonings: you will throw the recipe off balance and change the taste.

3. It is important to cut ingredients in uniform sizes for each recipe, as specified.

4. Always use cornstarch on the scant side.

5. Never stir-fry vegetables more than 3 minutes at the most.

6. Remember that ginger and garlic fry very rapidly—they never take longer than 30 seconds over low heat.

7. All recipes using stock can be made with canned, clear, chicken soup, any basic stock recipe, or chicken bouillon cubes, unless otherwise specified.

8. If you pound garlic with a cleaver, the skin will be easy to remove.

9. It is easier to cut meat when it is partially frozen.

10. To prevent lumping, always mix cornstarch in water with one finger.

11. To cook Virginia ham, place in a bowl on rack in pot or in steamer. Steam over boiling water 20 to 30 minutes, depending on the quantity. Always use precooked ham in these recipes.

12. Chop your ingredients in advance and have everything ready to use in separate bowls.

13. You can substitute Sweeta for sugar and arrowroot for corn-starch—although sugar and cornstarch are recommended.

14. Shrimp must be very fresh and purchased raw.

15. Measure every ingredient very carefully, using only the amount specified at the specified time.

16. Always use whole green bamboo shoots in recipes calling for bamboo shoots.

17. Many foods may be prepared in advance on the same day you are going to serve them. (Cutting and chopping may be done the day before.) Each recipe notes any special instructions and whether or not a prepared dish may be frozen and thawed, reheated, or refried before serving. However, for the best flavor cook foods just before serving.

2

Dim Sum, or Appetizers

Dim sum translated means a "dot to the heart," or a "small portion." They are Chinese finger foods and are used for hors d'oeuvres and entrées alike; the sweet ones are used for desserts. When you eat *dim sum,* you do not stuff yourself but eat just enough to touch the heart. They are easy to prepare and very popular in China, where we serve them with a pot of tea for breakfast, for lunch, and for early afternoon snacks.

Most of these delicacies are prepared with wheat. Lin Yu Tang, the great Chinese philosopher of the nineteenth century, said that rice develops brain and wheat develops brawn. In the north of China, wheat is the staple whereas in the south, rice is. Thus a Southerner can outwit a Northerner, but the latter can always beat up the former. In an age where might is still right, the South is taking to wheat!

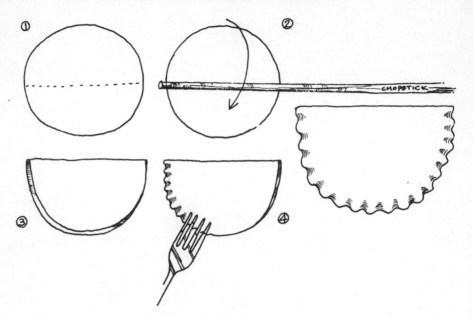

Buns (Basic Recipe)   ALL REGIONS

Western people are unaware that the Chinese have so many varieties of bread. They are served as snacks, for breakfast, for tea, and also as desserts. Buns can have any of several fillings. Bean paste, date paste, and sesame seed paste are sweet; barbecued pork, chicken, shrimp, and vegetables are salty. Buns are made in many different shapes. The following is the basic steamed bun recipe.

1 package dried yeast or
    1 cake fresh yeast
1 cup lukewarm water
4½ cups flour
¼ cup sugar

2 tablespoons Crisco or
    vegetable oil
½ cup boiling water
2 tablespoons sesame seed oil

1. Dissolve yeast in lukewarm water. Add 1 cup of flour. Mix thoroughly. Cover with cloth. Let rise 1 hour, until bubbles appear.
2. Dissolve sugar and vegetable oil in ½ cup boiling water. Stir well. Cool until lukewarm. Pour into yeast mixture. Add 3½ cups flour.
3. Knead dough on lightly floured board until smooth. Put into extra large, greased bowl in a warm place. Cover with damp cloth. Let rise until double in bulk, about 2 hours.

4. Divide into 2 portions.   Remove first portion and knead 2 minutes. Repeat with second.   Roll each into roll 12 inches long and 2 inches wide. Cut into 12 pieces (24 total).
5. Flatten each piece with palm of hand.   Roll with rolling pin into 3-inch circles.
6. Brush with sesame seed oil.   Indent middle of circle with chopstick.
7. Fold circle in half so that it becomes a half moon.   Crimp edges tightly with fork.
8. Place each roll on separate square piece of foil on steamer tray.   Cover tray with towel.   Let buns rise to double in bulk, about 30 minutes.   Remove towel.
9. Steam, tightly covered, over briskly boiling water for 10 minutes.   Serve with Peking Duck, Crispy Duck, or with any filling you desire.

May be prepared in advance.   May be frozen.   Thaw out in plastic bag and resteam 10 minutes.

24 Buns

Remember the three P's—patience, pride, and persistence.

Buns with Barbecued Pork Filling   CANTON

There is literally no end to the variety of fillings used in the traditional steamed buns that have made Chinese cooks famous. This popular filling is one of the best and is quick and easy to prepare. With practice, the process of pleating the dough around the filling becomes easier. When you can do it so there is a small lift in the middle of the top of the bun right where the pleats come together, consider yourself professional!

2 tablespoons oil

1 scallion, chopped fine

1 clove garlic, chopped fine

½ pound barbecued pork cut into small cubes

2 tablespoons light soy sauce

2 tablespoons oyster sauce

1 tablespoon sugar

1 tablespoon cornstarch, dissolved in 2 tablespoons water or chicken stock

1. Follow Basic Bun recipe through step 3.
2. Heat 2 tablespoons oil in wok. Stir-fry scallion and garlic 30 seconds. Add pork. Stir-fry 1 minute. Add soy sauce, oyster sauce, and sugar.
3. Pour in dissolved cornstarch. Stir-fry quickly until pork is glazed. Remove to bowl and allow to cool.
4. On a floured board, knead dough 1 minute and roll into one long, sausage-like roll 2 inches in diameter.
5. Slice the roll crosswise into 1-inch pieces.
6. Flatten each piece with the palm of your hand and roll with rolling pin into 3-inch rounds.
7. Place 2 tablespoons of filling in center of each round.
8. Gather dough up around the filling by pleating along the edges. Bring the pleats up and twist securely and firmly.
9. Place each bun on 2-inch square of aluminum foil on steamer tray. Cover with a towel. Let rise 1 hour, until dough springs back when touched with finger. Remove towel.
10. Steam over briskly boiling water 10 minutes.

May be prepared in advance. May be frozen. Thaw out in plastic bag and resteam 10 minutes.

24 Buns

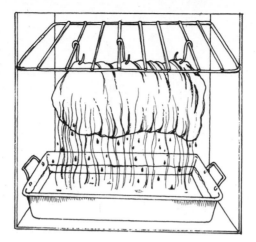

Barbecued Pork   CANTON

This pork dish is very famous in Canton. It can be used in stir-fried dishes, rice, and soup. It is good over noodles and as stuffing for buns, and it is marvelous with any beverage.

**1 pound pork tenderloin or
    shoulder**
2 tablespoons honey
3 tablespoons light soy sauce

1 teaspoon dark soy sauce
1 tablespoon sherry
1 clove garlic, mashed

1. Trim meat. Cut into strips about 2 inches wide and 6 inches long.
2. Combine remaining ingredients in bowl.
3. Marinate pork in this mixture 2 hours or longer.
4. Skewer pork with steel skewers. Hang skewers onto top rack of oven over shallow roasting pan containing a few inches of water.
5. Preheat oven to 425 degrees for 10 minutes. Roast pork 20 minutes. With baster, coat with drippings every 5 minutes. Reduce heat to 325 degrees and roast 5 minutes more.
6. Slice each strip diagonally against the grain into ¼-inch thick pieces. Serve cold.

May be prepared in advance. To freeze, wrap in foil.

Serves 4 to 6

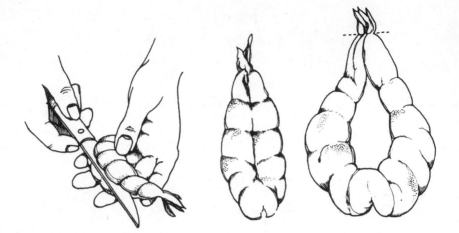

Butterfly Shrimp   CANTON

The butterfly is a symbol of blessings. We Chinese embroider butterflies on silk, we paint butterflies on scrolls and porcelain, and we make butterfly kites. We also butterfly our seafood.

1 pound shrimp (16 to 20), shelled and deveined
½ teaspoon salt
1 tablespoon flour
4 cups oil for deep-frying

Batter:

6 tablespoons flour
3 tablespoons cornstarch
½ teaspoon salt
Pinch of pepper
6 tablespoons water
1 teaspoon baking powder
¼ teaspoon soda

Sauce:

¼ cup tomato catsup
¼ cup sugar
¼ cup white vinegar
1 cup water
2 tablespoons cornstarch, dissolved in 2 tablespoons water
½ green pepper, cut into chunks

1. Wash shrimp. Dry on paper towel. With a sharp knife or scissors, make a slice down the backs of shrimp, leaving each end intact.
2. Sprinkle salt and flour evenly on shrimp.

3. To make batter: Mix flour, cornstarch, salt, and pepper. Stir in water. Add baking powder and soda. Beat until smooth.

4. To prepare sauce: Place first 4 ingredients in saucepan. Bring to boil. Thicken with dissolved cornstarch. Add green pepper. Bring to boil again. Remove from heat and set aside.

5. Heat oil to 375 degrees in wok. Dip shrimp into batter, one at a time. Drop shrimp into oil. Deep-fry until golden brown and crispy. Use chopstick to keep hole open. Drain on paper towel. Serve with sauce.

Shrimp may be cut and floured in advance. Do not freeze.

Serves 4 to 6

Fried Crab Claw   CANTON

This is an elegant banquet dish, and it is also an appealing appetizer.

¾ pound fresh shrimp,
    shelled and deveined
¾ teaspoon salt
Pepper to taste
1 tablespoon sherry

1 egg, well beaten
2 tablespoons cornstarch
10 raw crab claws*
4 tablespoons bread crumbs
2 to 4 cups oil for deep-frying

1. Boil crab claws in wok. Remove shell (leave 1 inch at the tip of the claw).

2. Finely chop shrimp by hand or use an electric blender. Add salt, pepper, sherry, ½ the beaten egg, and 1 teaspoon of cornstarch. Blend mixture.

3. Scoop 1½ tablespoons of shrimp mixture on each crab claw. Use wet fingers to shape mixture smoothly around it. Leave tip as handle. Dredge claws evenly with remaining cornstarch.

4. Dip claws in remaining ½ beaten egg. Coat evenly with bread crumbs.

5. Heat oil. When moderately hot, add crab claws. Deep fry about 12 minutes, until they become golden brown, turning occasionally. Drain on paper towel.

6. Serve with peppercorn salt (See Index) or any dip.

---

* If cooked crab claws are purchased, do not reboil.

May be prepared in advance through step 4. May be frozen after step 4.

Serves 10

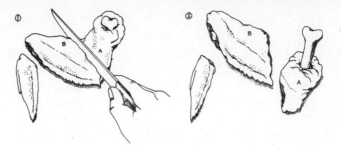

Chicken Sticks

6 chicken wings
1 teaspoon salt
Dash of pepper
1 teaspoon garlic powder
½ cup flour
4 cups oil for deep-frying

Batter:

¼ cup flour
2 tablespoons cornstarch
½ teaspoon baking powder
¼ teaspoon salt
Pinch of soda
½ cup cold water

1. To make wings look like drumsticks, cut off wing tips; break off joint from middle section and large section.
2. Remove small bone from middle section. Pull meat inside out.
3. Push all meat from large section to end of bones until it looks like a drumstick. Use knife to get the meat away from the bones if necessary.
4. Sprinkle with salt, pepper, and garlic powder. Coat with flour.
5. Mix all dry batter ingredients; then add water. Stir well with finger.
6. Heat oil to 375 degrees in wok. Dip floured sticks in batter. Deep-fry sticks until lightly brown. Serve with Sweet and Sour Sauce (See Index).

May be prepared in advance and refrigerated, or frozen after step 5.

12 Chicken Sticks

Chow-Tse (Meat Dumpling) (Fried)

ALL REGIONS

The Northerners eat a great deal of Chow-Tse. For them, it is a meal. Chow-Tse is also delightful as a snack. Chopped, blanched vegetables such as spinach, bok choy, or celery cabbage can be added to the filling.

Filling

1 pound ground pork, beef, or veal
1 teaspoon scallion, chopped fine
1 teaspoon ginger
4 ounces shrimp, shelled, deveined
    and chopped
1 tablespoon oil
½ teaspoon salt
2 tablespoons light soy sauce
1 tablespoon sherry
Pinch of sugar
¼ cup chicken stock

Dumplings

2 cups flour
⅔ cup lukewarm water
2 tablespoons oil
¾ cup chicken stock

1. Mix filling ingredients together in bowl. Set aside.
2. Pour lukewarm water into flour. Stir with fork or chopstick. Mix and knead into soft dough. Cover with damp cloth. Set aside 10 minutes.
3. Knead dough 1 minute. Roll into a long sausage. Cut into 1-inch lengths.
4. Sprinkle flour on board. Flatten each piece with rolling pin. Roll very thin, about 3 inches in diameter.
5. Place 1 tablespoon filling in center of each piece.
6. Fold over into half-moon shape. Pinch edges together at center. Make three pleats at each end. Pinch edges together to seal. Cover dumplings with a dry towel.
7. Grease frying pan with 1 tablespoon of oil. Arrange dumplings in rows, pleated side up. Cook over moderate heat about 3 minutes.
8. Pour stock around dumplings. Cover tightly. Continue cooking 10 minutes, or until dumplings are golden brown on the bottom.
9. Pour 1 tablespoon oil around dumplings. Let them fry uncovered 1 minute more.
10. Serve hot with red wine vinegar and shredded ginger.

May be prepared in advance. May be frozen after step 6.

24 Dumplings

Chow-Tse (Meat Dumpling) 　　　　　PEKING
(Steamed)

Here is a steamed version of Chow-Tse. The Pekingese also serve Chow-Tse as an entire meal; it contains all the ingredients for a well-balanced diet.

Dough

2 cups pre-sifted all-purpose flour
Pinch of salt
½ cup boiling water

1. Put flour into bowl. Add salt and boiling water.
2. Stir well with chopstick. Pour onto floured board. Knead 10 minutes, until dough is smooth and elastic.
3. Cover dough with a damp cloth. Let stand at least 10 minutes.
4. Roll dough into long sausage shape about 1 inch in diameter.
5. Cut dough into 24 pieces.
6. Each piece of dough must be rolled into a circular shape until it is very thin and 3 inches in diameter. The center must be thicker than the edges.

Filling

½ pound celery cabbage blanched in boiling water 1 minute, rinsed in cold	**1 teaspoon sherry**
	2 tablespoons cooked oil
½ pound minced pork	**1 teaspoon salt**
½ teaspoon ginger, chopped fine	**4 ounces shrimp, shelled, deveined, and chopped**
½ teaspoon scallion, chopped fine	
3 tablespoons light soy sauce	**2 tablespoons vinegar**
	2 tablespoons ginger, shredded

1. Wring cabbage in cloth to remove water. Chop fine.
2. Combine cabbage with pork, ginger, scallion, 2 tablespoons of soy sauce, sherry, oil, salt, and shrimp. Stir thoroughly until mixed.
3. Put 1 tablespoon of filling on each piece of dough.
4. Fold over into half-moon shape. Pinch edges together to seal. To be professional or fancy, one pleats the edge of the upper layer of Chow-Tse, then seals it together.
5. Place Chow-Tse on damp cloth on steamer tray. Steam over boiling water 10 minutes.
6. Combine 1 tablespoon soy sauce, vinegar, and shredded ginger. Serve with Chow-Tse immediately.

May be prepared in advance and refrigerated, or frozen after step 4.

24 Dumplings

Deep-Fried Walnut Chicken   PEKING

You may use this as an entrée or an hors d'oeuvre.

½ pound chicken breasts, boned
    and skinned
2 egg whites
1 teaspoon salt
Pepper to taste

¼ cup cornstarch
2 cups walnuts, coarsely chopped
2 to 4 cups oil for deep-frying
Sliced canned pineapple
Stemless maraschino cherries

1. Cut chicken breasts into bite-sized pieces.
2. Beat egg whites to soft peaks. Add salt and pepper. Sift cornstarch onto egg whites. Fold in gently.
3. Dip chicken pieces into egg white mixture.
4. Put walnuts on aluminum foil. Coat chicken evenly with walnuts.
5. Heat oil to 375 degrees in wok. Deep-fry chicken. Drop in a few pieces at a time. Fry until golden brown. Drain.
6. Place chicken on platter. Garnish with pineapple and cherries.
7. Serve with Fruity Fruity Sauce (See Index).

May be prepared in advance through step 4 and refrigerated. Do not freeze.

Serves 4 to 6

Always find time for love, find the time to hold hands with the one you love.

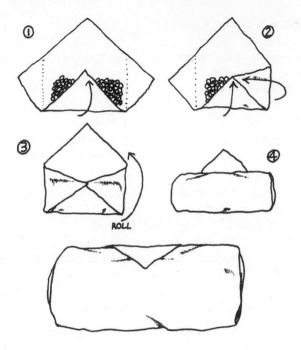

ROLL

Egg Roll

ALL REGIONS

The original name of this snack was Spring Roll. In China, it is usually served for the New Year because it is shaped like a 10-ounce gold bar, the symbol of wealth. Whenever it is offered to guests we say, "May you have prosperity for the coming year."

5 tablespoons oil
½ teaspoon ginger, chopped fine
1 scallion, chopped fine
½ pound pork shoulder or fillet, shredded or minced, mixed with 1 teaspoon oil and 1 teaspoon cornstarch
2 tablespoons light soy sauce
1 teaspoon sugar
½ cup shrimp (optional)
1½ teaspoons salt
½ teaspoon cornstarch
1 tablespoon sherry

½ head celery cabbage or regular cabbage, shredded
¼ cup bamboo shoots, shredded
¼ cup dried black mushrooms, soaked in boiling water 20 minutes, stems removed, shredded
¼ cup celery, julienne
½ pound bean sprouts
20 egg roll wrappings
1 tablespoon cornstarch, dissolved in 2 tablespoons water
4 cups oil for deep-frying

1. Heat 2 tablespoons oil in wok. Stir-fry ginger and scallion 30 seconds or until aroma comes. Add pork. Stir-fry 1 minute until color changes. Add 1 tablespoon of soy sauce and sugar. Cook 1 minute. Remove.

2. Mix shrimp with ½ teaspoon of salt and ½ teaspoon cornstarch. Stir-fry quickly. Add sherry. Stir-fry 1 second. Remove.

3. Heat 2 tablespoons oil in wok. Stir-fry cabbage, bamboo shoots, mushrooms, and celery 1 minute. Remove.

4. Heat 1 tablespoon oil in wok. Stir-fry bean sprouts 1 minute. Remove.

5. Combine pork, shrimp, and vegetable mixtures in wok. Add 1 teaspoon salt and 1 tablespoon soy sauce. Stir-fry until thoroughly heated. Remove to colander. Drain liquid. Cool mixture. Set aside, ready to be used as filling.

6. Put 2 heaping tablespoonsful of meat mixture on each wrapping. Roll lengthwise into envelopes about 4 inches long and 1 inch wide. Seal with dissolved cornstarch.

7. Heat 4 cups oil to 375 degrees in wok. Deep-fry 3 to 4 minutes, until golden brown. Serve with red wine vinegar or plum sauce.

NOTE: If shrimp are not used, add sherry after soy sauce in step 1.

May be prepared in advance through step 6. May be frozen after step 7. Reheat in oven or refry.

20 Egg Rolls

Embroidered Fish Balls   YANGCHOW

This is a priceless recipe created for the Imperial Palace. It is delicious served with beef and asparagus. The balls are "embroidered" because the hot oil creates a fancy pattern on the coated surface.

1 pound fillet of sole
1 ounce cooked Virginia ham
1 cup bok choy (Chinese green),
    leaves only, or 2 ounces
    spinach leaves
4 dried black mushrooms, soaked
    in boiling water 20 minutes,
    cooked 20 minutes, stems
    removed
1 bamboo shoot
1 teaspoon salt

2 tablespoons cornstarch (enough
    to form balls)
1 teaspoon dry sherry
1 egg
2 cups oil for deep-frying

Sauce (optional)

1 cup chicken stock
1 tablespoon cornstarch
1 tablespoon Virginia ham,
    minced

1. Into large bowl slice sole, ham, green leaves of bok choy or spinach, mushrooms, and bamboo shoot into julienne strips.
2. Mix with salt, cornstarch, sherry, and egg. If necessary, add more cornstarch and form into balls 1½ inches in diameter.
3. Heat oil to 375 degrees in wok. Drop in balls a few at a time. Deep-fry until color changes and remove. Drain.
4. Serve with peppercorn salt or the following sauce:
5. Sauce: Bring 1 cup chicken stock to boil. Thicken with 1 tablespoon dissolved cornstarch. Sprinkle with 1 tablespoon cooked minced Virginia ham.

May be prepared in advance and refrigerated after step 2. Do not freeze.

Serves 4 to 6

Fried Fragrant Bells   HANGCHOW

The crispness of the dried bean curd makes this dish crunchy. The shape of it is like a tiny bell. It makes an outstanding hors d'oeuvre.

1 pound ground pork, beef,	**1 tablespoon sherry**
chicken or veal	**1 egg**
2 scallions, chopped fine	**3 tablespoons chicken stock**
1 slice ginger, chopped fine	**4 dried bean curd sheets**
4 tablespoons cornstarch	**2 to 4 cups oil for deep-frying**
1 tablespoon dark soy sauce	**2 tablespoons peppercorn salt**

1. Combine meat with scallion, ginger, 1 tablespoon of cornstarch, soy sauce, sherry, egg, and stock. Mix thoroughly.
2. Place a bean curd sheet on a flat surface and moisten with warm water, just enough to dampen it.
3. Spoon ¼ of meat mixture onto sheet. Roll like a jelly roll. Repeat process with other three sheets.
4. Cut each roll into 1½-inch pieces.
5. Dip each end into remaining 3 tablespoons cornstarch to seal.
6. Heat oil to 375 degrees in wok. Deep-fry bells until crispy. Serve with peppercorn salt.

May be prepared in advance and refrigerated, or frozen after step 5.

32 Bells

This tastes like heaven above heaven.

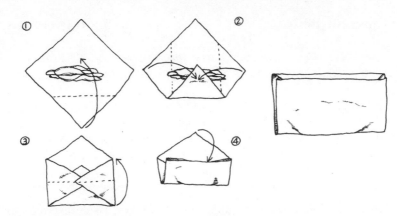

Gift-wrapped Chicken   ALL REGIONS

*In Hong Kong, an American free-lance writer interviewed me in June, 1961.
I presented him with this delicacy and suggested that it might be suitable for
American restaurants.   Since then this dish has appeared on menus
throughout the United States.*

1 pound chicken fillet	½ teaspoon salt
¼ cup oyster sauce	1 teaspoon sugar
2 tablespoons light soy sauce	24 sprigs of Chinese parsley
¼ cup sesame seed oil	(Celantro)
1 tablespoon sherry	24 6-inch squares of wax paper
½ teaspoon garlic juice	or aluminum foil
(use garlic press)	2 to 4 cups oil for deep-frying

1. Cut chicken fillet into 48 thin slices 1 inch wide, 2½ inches long, and ⅛-inch thick. Pound chicken gently with back of knife to tenderize.
2. Thoroughly mix liquid ingredients, salt, and sugar.   Add chicken.
Marinate 30 minutes.
3. On each square of paper or foil arrange a sprig of parsley and two pieces
of chicken. Wrap and fold like an envelope and tuck in the ends.
4. Bring oil to boil in wok. Lower heat to moderate. Deep-fry wrapped
chicken 3 minutes several pieces at a time. Turn constantly with chopsticks.
5. Reheat oil between frying each batch of chicken.

May be prepared in advance and refrigerated, or frozen after step 3.

24 Chicken Packages

Pearl Balls   HANGCHOW

Country people around Hangchow make this dish for the New Year. A meatball, being round, signifies reunion in the Chinese language. Use this as an appetizer or an entrée.

1 cup glutinous sweet rice	**1 tablespoon sherry**
1 pound ground pork	**2 tablespoons light soy sauce**
1 egg white	**2 tablespoons water**
1 teaspoon salt	

1. Wash rice. Let soak overnight. Drain. Rice should be dry when ready to use. Set aside.
2. Combine remaining ingredients. Stir well. Take about 1 tablespoon mixture to form each of 24 balls.
3. Roll very lightly onto rice so that rice barely coats each ball. Sprinkle more rice on top. Repeat process for each ball.
4. Place meatballs on plate. Place on rack in pot. Cover and steam over boiling water 30 minutes.

May be prepared in advance through step 3. May be frozen after step 4. Resteam before serving.

24 Pearl Balls

Scallion Cake   PEKING

This cake can be served as bread, as an appetizer, or with tea. It is also wonderful to serve with Meatball Soup or any other hot soup for dinner.

1 cup flour	2 teaspoons salt
½ cup water	4 scallions, chopped fine
2 tablespoons Crisco	2 tablespoons vegetable oil

1. Put flour on board. Make a well in the center. Add water. Mix into soft, smooth dough. Divide into 2 portions.
2. Roll each portion very thin.
3. Brush each with 1 tablespoon Crisco. Sprinkle with 1 teaspoon salt. Spread half the scallions evenly on each sheet.
4. Roll like a snail, or jelly roll.
5. Then coil it. Flatten with rolling pin until it is 7 inches in diameter.
6. Heat 1 tablespoon oil. Fry cake over medium heat 2 minutes on each side. Repeat.
7. Cut each cake into 8 portions and serve.

May be prepared in advance of frying. Cakes may be frozen after step 6 but refry or reheat in oven 10 minutes before slicing and serving.

16 Cakes

Shao Mai   ALL REGIONS

My students get excited when they prepare this recipe. It can be served as an appetizer and is extremely good with Fried Eight Pieces.

1 pound ground pork, ground beef, or chopped shrimp	**½ teaspoon salt**
1 tablespoon sherry	**4 water chestnuts, chopped fine**
2 tablespoons light soy sauce	**1 teaspoon cornstarch**
1 scallion, chopped fine	**24 pieces Shao Mai or won ton wrappings**

1. In bowl combine meat or shrimp with all other ingredients except wrappings. Mix well.
2. Put 1 tablespoon of filling in center of each wrapping. Gather sides of each wrapping around filling. Squeeze center gently. Leave edges of dough shirred.
3. Line steamer tray with wet cloth. Place Shao Mai on tray over boiling water. Steam 20 minutes.
4. After steaming, remove Shao Mai to platter at once to prevent sticking. May be served with red wine vinegar or a combination of equal parts of red wine vinegar and light soy sauce.

May be prepared completely in advance and resteamed. You may freeze them after step 2 and then steam them 30 minutes before serving.

24 Shao Mai

Shrimp Toast

This dish can be served as an appetizer or it can be one of several dishes for a Chinese banquet. It is best served immediately after deep-frying. If necessary, it can be kept warm in a 200-degree oven for about 15 minutes.

9 slices of extra-thin white bread (day old preferable)
Water
1 pound fresh shrimp, shelled, deveined, and chopped
4 water chestnuts, chopped fine
½ medium-sized onion, chopped fine
1 scallion, chopped fine
1 teaspoon salt
1 teaspoon sherry
1 tablespoon cornstarch
1 egg, slightly beaten
Pepper to taste
2 to 4 cups oil for deep-frying

1. Trim crusts from bread. Cut each slice into 4 squares (36 squares).
2. Soak 4 of the squares in water 1 second. Squeeze out liquid. Set all aside.
3. In a bowl combine shrimp, water chestnuts, onion, scallion, salt, sherry, cornstarch, egg, pepper, and soaked bread squares. Mix well.
4. Place 1 teaspoon of shrimp mixture on each of remaining bread squares, slightly mounded.
5. Heat oil to 375 degrees in wok. Slide bread pieces into oil, a few at a time, with shrimp side down.
6. Deep-fry about 1 minute. Turn and fry other side until golden brown.
7. Drain on paper towels.

May be prepared through step 4 and refrigerated or frozen.

32 Shrimp Toasts

Spareribs
(Fried)   PEKING

These ribs are different from the traditional American type. The sauce is another great favorite of all my students; the only problem is to stop your guests from filling up on these before the rest of the dinner arrives. This dish goes well with Shrimp with Peas.

1 pound baby back spareribs	1 egg
Boiling water	¼ cup flour
4 pieces of scallion tops,	2 to 4 cups oil for deep-frying
cut in 1-inch strips	¼ cup sugar
3 tablespoons dark soy sauce	¼ cup wine vinegar

1. Cut spareribs into 1-inch pieces. Place in a pot with boiling water to cover. Add scallion. Boil 10 minutes. Drain and remove scallion. Cool ribs.
2. Add 1 tablespoon of soy sauce, egg, and flour to spareribs. Mix well.
3. Heat oil to 375 degrees in wok. Deep-fry ribs until very brown, about 3 to 5 minutes. Remove.
4. In saucepan, heat 2 tablespoons soy sauce, sugar, and vinegar. Stir until thick. Toss spareribs in this mixture until they are thoroughly glazed.

May be prepared in advance and refrigerated or frozen. Thaw and reheat in oven on cookie sheet 20 minutes before serving.

Serves 4 to 6

Success means competition.

Spareribs   CANTON
(Oven-Baked)

Many of my students make a meal of these.

2 tablespoons dark soy sauce   1 clove garlic, chopped fine
2 tablespoons light soy sauce   1 tablespoon sugar
2 tablespoons honey   Aluminum foil
3 tablespoons hoisin sauce   2 pounds spareribs, cut into
1 tablespoon sherry   3 pieces lengthwise
1 tablespoon tomato catsup

1. Combine all ingredients but meat in shallow dish/pan. Add spareribs. Marinate overnight, turning several times.
2. Line shallow pan with aluminum foil. Preheat oven to 350 degrees. Roast spareribs 45 minutes. Turn heat to 325 degrees. Roast 15 minutes more. (When shrinkage occurs, ribs are finished.)

May be prepared in advance and refrigerated or frozen. Thaw and reheat 20 minutes.

Serves 4 to 6

Don't count the good deeds you have done for others. Count the kindnesses people have done for you, then you will be more appreciative.

Stuffed Mushrooms with Oyster Sauce   CANTON

This is an elegant hors d' oeuvre. Serve with mustard.

20 dried black mushrooms
1½ cups boiling water
½ pound minced pork, beef, or
    any seafood
½ teaspoon salt
2 tablespoons oil plus
    1 teaspoon
1 teaspoon sugar

1 tablespoon sherry
1 tablespoon light soy sauce
1 teaspoon cornstarch
4 sprigs Chinese parsley
    (Celantro)
1 cup mushroom stock
2 tablespoons oyster sauce

1. Wash mushrooms and remove stems. Soak in boiling water 1 hour. Cook 1 hour on low heat. Reserve 1 cup water for stock. Drain mushrooms and dry.
2. Combine meat or seafood with salt, 1 teaspoon of oil, ½ teaspoon of sugar, sherry, soy sauce, and cornstarch. Mix well with hand.
3. Sprinkle a little cornstarch on inside of each mushroom (this will make mixture stick).
4. Put 1 tablespoon of meat mixture in mushroom and garnish with parsley leaves.
5. Fry mushrooms in 2 tablespoons oil, meat side down, until meat turns lightly brown. Turn, add mushroom stock, and cook 10 minutes. Add oyster sauce and ½ teaspoon sugar. Cook over high heat 1 minute until gravy thickens and coats the mushrooms.

May be prepared in advance through step 4. May be frozen after step 5. Reheat in wok with 4 tablespoons chicken stock.

20 Stuffed Mushrooms

Turnip Cake   CANTON

This is a more glorified version of potato cake. Everybody loves it, and turnips are so nourishing.

2½ pounds turnips
1 cup water
2 cups long-grain rice flour
5 tablespoons oil
1 tablespoon scallion,
    chopped fine
4 dried black mushrooms, soaked in
    boiling water 20 minutes,
    stems removed, cooked 20
    minutes, chopped fine

¼ cup dried shrimp, chopped fine,
    soaked in 1 tablespoon sherry
4 Chinese sausages, chopped fine
2 teaspoons salt
½ teaspoon sugar
½ teaspoon pepper
1 tablespoon Chinese parsley
    (Celantro), chopped fine
1 tablespoon sesame seeds,
    toasted (See Index)

1. Peel and grate turnips. Simmer in 1 cup water about 1 hour, or until tender.
2. Mix rice flour and turnips in bowl until consistency of thick oatmeal. Add 2 tablespoons of oil. Mix well. Set aside.
3. Heat 2 tablespoons oil in wok. Stir-fry scallion, mushrooms, shrimps and sausages and add to turnip mixture.
4. Add salt, sugar, and pepper. Mix thoroughly.
5. Grease a 6″ × 9″ cake pan. Pour mixture into it. Sprinkle with parsley and sesame seeds. Place on rack in steamer. Steam over briskly boiling water 1 hour.
6. When cold, refrigerate overnight.
7. To serve, slice ¼-inch thick, 2 inches wide, and 3 inches long. Fry slices in 1 tablespoon oil until golden brown. Serve hot.

May be prepared in advance and refrigerated after step 6. Slice and fry before serving. May be frozen after step 5.

Serves 4 to 6

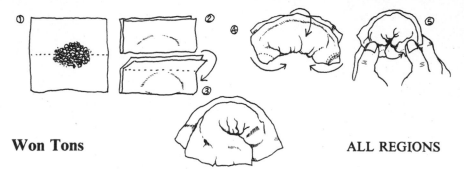

Won Tons   ALL REGIONS

Won tons are such a versatile dish. They may be served as a one-dish meal or at tea time; you can fry them for cocktails or make them into a soup. Any leftovers may be pan-fried the following day for another tour of duty.

½ pound ground pork*
½ teaspoon salt
1 tablespoon light soy sauce
1 tablespoon sherry
4 water chestnuts, chopped fine
1 scallion, chopped fine
½ egg, beaten

2 leaves of bok choy
    (Chinese green), optional
60 won ton wrappings
    (purchase in Chinese
    markets)
2 to 4 cups oil for deep-frying

1. Combine pork with salt, soy sauce, sherry, water chestnuts, scallion, beaten egg, and bok choy. (If using bok choy, dip it into boiling water, boil 1 minute. Drain. Squeeze out water and chop fine.) Mix well. This is the won ton filling.

2. Put 1 teaspoon of filling in center of each wrapping. Fold to the center. Gently press edges together. Fold in half again lengthwise; then fold back and bring ends together.

3. Dab a little water on one corner, put two corners one over the other, and press together. Won ton properly made resembles a nurse's cap.

4. Heat oil to 375 degrees in wok. Deep-fry won tons 2 minutes. Drain. Serve with Sweet Sour Sauce (See Index).

---

* Beef, veal, turkey, chicken, or crab meat may be used in place of pork. (See Index for recipe for Won Ton Soup).

May be prepared in advance through step 3, or frozen after step 3. Deep-fry when they are at room temperature.

60 Won Tons

3

Soups

Soup plays an important role in any Chinese meal. For family meals it is served as a last course. At banquets, various soups are served between courses. I have included many delicious and interesting soup recipes because they are part of the symphony of a well-planned meal.

A good soup depends upon good, basic stock; and each recipe assumes you have it. A properly made stock will help to enrich your soup without adding calories or fat.

Basic Chicken Stock   ALL REGIONS

Although canned chicken stock can be used in recipes, a good homemade stock is always richer and more wholesome. You can bottle it and it will keep in the refrigerator about five days. If you wish to keep it longer, reheat it, cool it again, and replace in the refrigerator. You can also freeze stock indefinitely. Use this recipe wherever stock is indicated in a recipe unless otherwise specified.

12 cups water   2 pieces ginger, ⅛-inch thick
1 whole chicken, about 3 to 4   1 tablespoon sherry
    pounds*
1 scallion

1. Bring water to boil in kettle. Add chicken, scallion, ginger, and sherry. As soon as it comes to a boil, turn off the heat and skim off foam.
2. Bring to boil again. Simmer 4 hours.
3. When stock is cool, strain and discard chicken.
4. Refrigerate overnight in bottles. Skim off fat from jellied stock and discard.

------

* Bones and carcass may be used in place of whole chicken.

Approximately 10 cups Basic Stock

An old pot is the best around the kitchen.

Chicken Soup with Stuffed Birds' Nests YANGCHOW

This is a banquet soup, a delicacy in Chinese cooking. Poor men dream of it and rich men eat it. These are the actual nests of the sea swallows. The swallows eat seaweeds and other sea plants and then make their nests by spitting out the gelatin-like substance the plants become. In old China rich families employed young girls with perfect vision to remove feathers from these nests—this was their only job. Today the birds' nests come precleaned. The Chinese believe birds' nests produce long life, good health, and energy.

4 balls birds' nests
Water
8 cups chicken stock
1 3-pound stewing chicken, cleaned
2 teaspoons salt
1 slice ginger, ⅛-inch thick

1 stalk scallion
1 tablespoon sherry
4 slices Virginia ham, 2½ inches
**   long, 2 inches wide,**
**   and ⅛-inch thick**

1. Soak birds' nests in water to cover overnight. Drain. Immerse in fresh water. Drain thoroughly. Bring birds' nests to boil in 2 cups of stock. Simmer 30 minutes. Discard stock. Set nests aside.
2. Rub chicken inside with 1 teaspoon of salt. Pound ginger to soften. Squeeze ginger juice inside chicken and rub ginger outside.
3. Stuff birds' nests into chicken. Sew up. Plunge chicken into pot of boiling water. Remove and drain.
4. Bring 6 cups stock to boil. Add scallion and chicken. Simmer 1 hour. Season with 1 teaspoon salt and sherry.
5. Bring to boil. Remove to large serving platter. Garnish with ham.

May be prepared in advance, or frozen after step 4. Bring to room temperature and complete.

Serves 6

Crab Meat and Asparagus Soup   ALL REGIONS

This pleasant and palatable soup is a great favorite of Western people.

6 cups chicken stock
1 teaspoon salt
1 teaspoon ginger, minced
1 can of white asparagus,
    cut into 1-inch pieces
1 cup flaked crab meat
1 tablespoon sherry

1 tablespoon light soy sauce
2 tablespoons cornstarch, dissolved
    in 4 tablespoons water
2 eggs, beaten slightly
1 scallion, chopped fine
pepper to taste

1. Bring stock to boil. Add salt and ginger.
2. Add asparagus and crab meat. Bring to boil. Add sherry and soy sauce.
3. Simmer 2 minutes. Stir in dissolved cornstarch. Cook 30 seconds.
4. Add eggs, stirring constantly in circular motion. Remove to tureen.
5. Sprinkle chopped scallion and pepper on top.

May be prepared in advance through step 4. May be frozen after step 5. Reheat and garnish with chopped scallion before serving.

Serves 6

Egg Dumpling Soup   SHANGHAI

This is a wholesome, hearty soup that can also serve as a one-dish meal. It is beautiful and appealing.

4 ounces vermicelli (mung bean)
½ pound ground pork
1 teaspoon salt
2 tablespoons light soy sauce
1 teaspoon cornstarch
5 eggs

1 tablespoon oil
8 cups chicken stock
1 bunch spinach, stems removed
1 tablespoon sesame seed oil
1 teaspoon pepper oil (optional)

1. Soak vermicelli in boiling water 20 minutes. Drain. Cut in half with scissors. Set aside.
2. Combine pork, ½ teaspoon of salt, 1 tablespoon of soy sauce, cornstarch, and 1 egg. Mix well. Set aside.
3. Beat 4 eggs lightly.

4. Pour oil into heavy skillet (about 8 inches) over moderate heat. Turn skillet to coat with oil. Pour in half the beaten eggs. Quickly whirl the pan around. Pancake will form in 30 seconds. As soon as it is set, lift up pancake with spatula. Remove. Repeat with remaining beaten eggs to make second pancake.

5. Divide meat mixture in half. Spread on each pancake. Roll like jelly roll. Seal edges with uncooked egg left in bowl.

6. Place these rolls on plate. Put plate on rack in pot or in steamer. Steam covered over boiling water 20 minutes.

7. Remove. Cut rolls diagonally into ½-inch slices.

8. Pour stock into wok or pot. Bring to boil. Add vermicelli. Place sliced pancake rolls on top. Bring to boil. Add 1 tablespoon soy sauce and ½ teaspoon salt.

9. Arrange spinach leaves around edge of wok or pot, forming a green circle. Add sesame seed oil. Bring to boil. If you prefer more spice, add 1 teaspoon pepper oil.

10. Remove to tureen, arranging spinach leaves in circle.

May be prepared in advance through step 7, or frozen after step 9.

Serves 6

Hot And Sour Soup   PEKING

An extraordinary and sustaining soup of marvelous flavor, full of vitamins and protein. Serve in a tureen after a football game or after the theater; this is perfect for a winter evening. It is beautiful and nourishing enough to solo as an early supper, with a compote of chilled lychees and kumquats for dessert. It is also delicious with Moo Shu Pork.

4 dried black mushrooms
¼ cup dried fungus
Boiling water
½ cup lean pork
½ cup bamboo shoots
½ teaspoon salt
1 teaspoon cornstarch
2 tablespoons oil
6 cups chicken stock
2 tablespoons light soy sauce

½ teaspoon pepper
3 tablespoons vinegar
2 tablespoons cornstarch, dissolved
    in ¼ cup water
2 pieces fresh bean curd,
    cut into thin strips
2 eggs, beaten
1 tablespoon sesame seed oil
2 scallions, cut into 1-inch
    lengths

1. Put mushrooms and fungus into separate bowls. Cover each with boiling water. Let soak 3 or 4 hours or overnight. Remove stems from mushrooms. Remove woody parts from fungus.
2. Separately cut mushrooms, fungus, pork, and bamboo shoots to fine julienne.
3. Mix pork with salt and cornstarch in bowl.
4. Stir-fry pork in heated oil.
5. Bring chicken stock to boil in pot. Add mushrooms, fungus, pork, and bamboo shoots. Stir constantly.
6. Add soy sauce, pepper, and vinegar. Thicken with dissolved cornstarch, stirring constantly over moderate heat.
7. Add bean curd. Bring to boil.
8. Turn off heat. Add beaten eggs. Stir quickly 30 seconds. Add sesame seed oil. Remove to tureen and garnish with scallions. Serve hot.

NOTE: Add more vinegar and pepper if a spicier taste is desired.

May be prepared in advance, or frozen after step 6. Bring to room temperature and complete.

Serves 6

Jade Soup   YANGCHOW

This soup is as beautiful to look at as it is exquisite to taste.

**1 whole chicken breast, boned
   and skinned**
4½ cups chicken stock
2 egg whites
1 tablespoon cornstarch
2 teaspoons salt

12 spinach leaves
2 tablespoons oil
1 tablespoon sherry
**2 tablespoons cornstarch,
   dissolved in 2 tablespoons
   water**

1. Chop chicken very fine or put in blender. Soak chopped chicken in ½ cup of stock.
2. Beat egg whites stiff. Gently fold in cornstarch, chicken, and 1 teaspoon of salt. Set aside.
3. Cook spinach in boiling water. Drain well. Squeeze out water. Chop very fine.
4. Heat oil in wok. Stir-fry spinach 10 seconds. Pour remaining 4 cups stock and sherry over spinach. Bring to boil.
5. Add chicken mixture. Bring to boil, stirring rapidly. Season with 1 teaspoon salt. Thicken with dissolved cornstarch.

May be prepared in advance. May be frozen. Reheat before serving.

Serves 6

No! No! No! I never use monosodium glutamate.

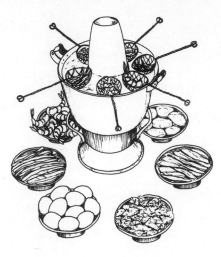

Mongolian Hot Pot
ALL REGIONS

Here is an ideal dish to serve during the winter months. It is interesting because the guests do their own cooking. A wonderful way to entertain—so relaxing for the host or hostess. It is a great favorite of both East and West.

1 whole chicken breast,
    boned and skinned
1 pound lean pork
1 pound flank steak
2 pounds fish fillet (red snapper
    or carp)
1 pound fresh large shrimps,
    shelled, deveined, cut
    into halves lengthwise
12 clams, shelled and cleaned
2 cups oil for deep frying
4 ounces vermicelli (mung bean)
8 cups chicken stock (more if
    needed)

8 cups water
2 tablespoons sherry
1 large head celery cabbage,
    cut into 1-inch strips
2 bunches spinach
10 eggs
salt to taste

Sauce

2 tablespoons light soy sauce
1 tablespoon sesame seed oil
⅛ teaspoon chili paste with
    garlic (optional)

1. Cut chicken, pork, flank steak, and fish into thin slices. Arrange on platter.
2. Place shrimps and clams on separate platters.

3. Heat oil to 375 degrees for deep-frying. Deep-fry vermicelli 1 second. Set aside.

4. Arrange the three platters of uncooked foods around a Chinese hot pot. If not available, use a chafing dish or electric wok.

5. Preheat stock. Add water and sherry. Pour into pot and keep simmering.

6. Cabbage, spinach, and vermicelli may be eaten after the meat. Poach eggs in stock last.

7. To serve, dip uncooked meats and vegetables into stock long enough to cook them. Then dip into sauce. (Put sauce in individual bowls.)

NOTE: If using Mongolian pot, heat charcoal briquets on a foil-lined baking pan under broiler for 20 minutes. Then place hot coals (20 side by side) in hot pot.

Do not prepare in advance. Do not freeze.

Serves 10

Meatball Soup   ALL REGIONS

This is the simplest most nourishing soup of all.

2 ounces vermicelli (mung bean)	1 tablespoon light soy sauce
1 pound ground pork	2 to 4 cups oil for deep-frying
1 scallion, chopped fine	6 cups chicken stock
1 egg	1 tablespoon sesame seed oil
1 teaspoon salt	1 scallion, chopped into 1-inch
1½ teaspoons cornstarch	pieces
1 tablespoon sherry	

1. Soften vermicelli in boiling water 20 minutes. Drain. Cut into 4-inch lengths. Set aside.

2. Mix pork with scallion, egg, salt, cornstarch, sherry, and soy sauce. Beat thoroughly. Shape into balls about the size of walnuts.

3. Heat oil in wok, to smoking hot. Put balls in one at a time. Deep-fry 5 minutes. Drain.

4. Bring stock to boil in pot. Add vermicelli and meat balls. Add sesame seed oil and scallion. Boil 1 minute.

May be prepared in advance. May be frozen. Reheat before serving.

Serves 6

Sour and Peppery Fish Chowder   PEKING

This is a highly seasoned soup, typical of the region.

1 pound fish fillet
1½ teaspoons salt
1 tablespoon sherry
1 teaspoon ginger, thinly sliced
6 cups chicken stock
1 teaspoon pepper
2 tablespoons red wine vinegar

2 tablespoons light soy sauce
2 tablespoons cornstarch,
    dissolved in ¼ cup water
2 tablespoons parsley, chopped
    fine
2 eggs, beaten

1. Rub fish with 1 teaspoon of salt. Put fish into bowl. Pour sherry over it. Add ginger.
2. Place bowl on rack in pot or in steamer. Steam covered over boiling water 10 minutes.
3. Remove fish bones and skin. Shred fish. Set aside.
4. Bring stock to boil in pot. Season with ½ teaspoon salt, pepper, vinegar, and soy sauce.
5. Thicken with dissolved cornstarch. Add parsley. Cook 30 seconds. Add fish, then beaten eggs. Stir quickly. Bring to boil and season to taste.

May be prepared in advance and refrigerated after step 4. Do not freeze.

Serves 6

Won Ton Soup   ALL REGIONS

Won ton soup is a meal in itself. I call it "family-and-friend reunion dish." Chicken, beef, or shrimp may be substituted for barbecued pork.

12½ cups water
½ recipe of ready-made raw
    won tons
6 cups chicken stock
¼ teaspoon salt
1 tablespoon light soy sauce

½ head bok choy (Chinese green),
    sliced thin
1 scallion, cut into 1-inch pieces
½ pound barbecued pork,
    sliced thin
1 tablespoon sesame seed oil

1. In large pot, bring 12 cups of water to boil. Add won tons. Bring to boil again. Add remaining water. Bring to boil once more. When won tons

float to surface, they are ready to be removed to strainer. Rinse under cold water. Drain. Set aside.

2. Bring stock to boil in wok or pot. Add salt, soy sauce, and bok choy. Boil 1 minute. Add scallion and barbecued pork. Drop won tons gently into soup from strainer. Add sesame seed oil. Boil 1 minute.

May be prepared in advance through step 1. Do not freeze.

Serves 6

Soybean Pudding Soup   ALL REGIONS

Those who are calorie-conscious can enjoy this light soup. Soybean pudding is fine, fresh bean curd, light as air, incredibly simple to cook. When I was a child growing up in China, peddlers who carried their wares and cooking equipment on a broad bamboo stick sang their songs and sold soybean pudding in the streets. All the children would gather around them after school, eager to exchange their pennies for afternoon snacks.

2 cups chicken stock
1 12-ounce package soybean
    pudding
2 tablespoons light soy sauce
¼ cup Szechwan preserved
    vegetable, washed and chopped
    fine

½ cup fresh shrimp, shelled,
    deveined, cut into quarters
1 tablespoon sesame seed oil
½ teaspoon pepper oil (optional)

1. Bring stock to boil in saucepan. Add soybean pudding, soy sauce, and preserved vegetable. Add shrimp. Bring to boil again.

2. Add sesame seed oil and pepper oil (if used) just before serving.

May be prepared in advance through step 1. Do not freeze.

Serves 6

Protein rich soya bean—we Chinese have had it 5,000 years.

Three-flavored Sizzling Rice Soup   YANGCHOW

Sizzling rice is the crust of the cooked rice. When it is deep fried it can be served as an hors d'oeuvre and in many other dishes.

½ cup black dried mushrooms,
   stems removed
½ cup chicken breast, sliced thin
¼ cup pork, sliced thin
Boiling water
6 cups chicken stock
1 cup mushroom stock
¼ cup bamboo shoots, sliced thin

½ cup pea pods (snow peas)
¼ cup fresh shrimp, shelled,
   deveined, cut into quarters
1 teaspoon salt
1 tablespoon light soy sauce
1 tablespoon sesame seed oil
2 to 4 cups oil for deep-frying
2 cups Rice Crispy Snack (See
   Index)

1. Soak mushrooms in boiling water 1 hour. Simmer in the liquid 1 hour more. Strain liquid carefully into a bowl. Reserve 1 cup. Discard residue. Quarter mushrooms. Set aside.
2. Put chicken and pork into boiling water. Cook until color changes. Rinse in cold water until clear. Drain.
3. Add stock to mushroom stock in saucepan. Boil. Add chicken and pork, mushrooms, and bamboo shoots. Then add pea pods and shrimp. Bring to boil again.
4. Season with salt and soy sauce. Add sesame seed oil. Bring to boil. Remove to tureen or bowl.
5. Heat oil in wok to smoking hot. Add Rice Crispy Snack. Deep-fry until it puffs and becomes golden brown. Drain.
6. Pour sizzling rice into soup.

May be prepared in advance through step 2. Do not freeze.

Serves 6

Three Shreds Shark's Fin Soup   ALL REGIONS

Shark's fin is like caviar to the Chinese, and the highest in quality may seem just as precious. Serve this soup when you wish to honor distinguished guests. The Dowager Empress ordered shark's fin soup daily because she believed in its great nutritional value. She also believed it kept her young.

½ pound shark's fin needle
10 cups water
2 slices ginger
4 scallions
8 cups chicken stock
2 tablespoons sherry
1 cup chicken fillet, julienne
½ egg white
½ teaspoon salt
1 teaspoon cornstarch
½ cup bamboo shoots, julienne

4 dried black mushrooms, soaked
    in boiling water 20 minutes,
    stems removed, cooked 20
    minutes, julienne
¼ cup cooked Virginia ham,
    julienne
2 tablespoons light soy sauce
2 tablespoons cornstarch
    dissolved in ¼ cup water
Pepper to taste
1 teaspoon red wine vinegar
Chinese parsley (Celantro)

1. Soak shark's fin needle in water to cover overnight. Drain.
2. Rinse shark's fin gently in a strainer. Put into pot. Add 8 cups of water, ginger, and scallions. Bring to boil. Simmer 2 hours. Drain. Discard ginger and scallions.
3. Cover shark's fin with 2 cups of chicken stock in pot. Add 2 cups water and sherry. Bring to boil. Simmer 30 minutes. Drain. Set aside. Discard liquid.
4. Combine chicken with egg white, salt, and cornstarch. Mix well with hand. Set aside.
5. Bring 6 cups chicken stock to boil in pot. Add shark's fin, bamboo shoots, mushrooms, and ham. Stir well. Bring to boil. Add chicken mixture. Bring to boil again. Add soy sauce. Thicken with dissolved cornstarch. Season with pepper. Add vinegar. Garnish with Chinese parsley. Serve hot from tureen.

May be prepared in advance and refrigerated or frozen.

Serves 6

Three Shreds Soup   ALL REGIONS

This soup started off with three kinds of shreds centuries ago—chicken, ham, and bamboo. As time went on, other delectable shreds were added to enrich the soup. The triplet has become a quintuplet!

1 teaspoon oil
1 whole dried black mushroom,
    soaked in boiling water 20
    minutes, cleaned, stem
    removed
1 cup cooked chicken, shredded
5 dried black mushrooms, soaked
    in boiling water 20 minutes,
    stems removed, shredded

½ cup cooked pork, shredded
9 bamboo shoots, shredded
½ cup cooked ham, shredded
2 teaspoons salt
6 cups chicken stock plus 2
    tablespoons
1 tablespoon sherry

1. Grease a small bowl with oil. Put whole mushroom in center of bowl, stem end up.
2. Arrange shredded chicken, mushrooms, pork, bamboo shoots, and ham in 5 sections around mushroom in bowl. Sprinkle with 1 teaspoon of salt. Pour in 2 tablespoons of stock. Place bowl on rack in pot or in steamer. Cover and steam over boiling water 20 minutes.
3. Heat 6 cups stock in pot. Add 1 teaspoon salt and sherry. Bring to boil.
4. When ready to serve, put a large serving soup bowl over the smaller bowl. Invert quickly. Pour soup in slowly from edge so as not to disturb the design.

May be prepared in advance, or frozen after step 2.

Serves 6

No medicine can cure stupidity.

Winter Melon Soup   ALL REGIONS

This is an elegant soup. Graceful and pretty, it really exemplifies the art of Chinese cooking.

1 5- to 6-pound winter melon, about 8 inches in diameter
¼ cup dried lotus seeds, soaked
¼ cup bamboo shoots, diced
4 dried black mushrooms, soaked in boiling water 20 minutes, stems removed, diced
1 cup water
1 chicken breast, diced
4 tablespoons Virginia ham, cooked and diced
1 tablespoon sherry
6 cups chicken stock
Salt to taste
Pepper to taste

1. Wash surface of winter melon thoroughly. Cut about 1/5 of melon off the top. Scrape out seeds and pulp.
2. Set melon in deep bowl that will hold it in place.
3. Set entire bowl in pot of water (water level not quite to top of bowl). Cover. Steam about 2 hours, checking water level constantly until melon is translucent.
4. Simmer lotus seeds, bamboo shoots, and mushrooms in 1 cup water in saucepan for 30 minutes. Add chicken breast and ham. Cook 3 minutes. Skim. Add sherry. Pour in stock. Bring to boil. Season with salt and pepper to taste.
5. Remove winter melon in bowl from pot of water. Pour stock and all ingredients into melon. It is a good idea to serve melon standing in bowl to prevent tipping.

May be prepared in advance. Resteam before serving. Do not freeze.

Serves 6

4

Chicken

Have you ever heard the Chinese expression, "The chicken is flying all over the table"? This simply means that one meal is served with chicken cooked five different ways. A cook who has culinary skills and resourcefulness can do this. The neck and feet are used to make the stock for bean curd soup. The breast can be sliced and stir-fried with vegetables; the legs boiled, chopped, and eaten with soy sauce; the back and wings braised with bamboo shoots in oyster sauce; and the fat of the chicken cooked with celery cabbage—five dishes, all told. We have hundreds of recipes for chicken.

When you buy chicken, be sure the skin is a rich yellow color and the breast is plump. It is best to cook chicken the same day you buy it.

Beggar's Chicken   KIANGSU

On the bank of a creek a ragged beggar sat sunning himself. Suddenly a chicken emerged from a farmhouse. Without the least hesitation, the beggar pounced upon his prey and wrung its neck to quiet the cackle. He was all set for a chicken dinner. But how? He had no knife to cut open his fowl nor any facility on which to cook. He came upon a bright idea.

He covered the chicken with mud and water. Then he gathered enough twigs to build a fire. When the fire began to roar, he threw in his loot. When the chicken was cooked, he cracked the covering and the feathers came off with the baked clay. He had a fine meal—imaginative gourmets have used his idea for this superb recipe!

1 2½- to 3-pound fryer chicken
2 teaspoons salt
1 teaspoon ginger juice (use garlic
    press or pound with back
    of knife)
4 tablespoons oil
1 scallion, chopped fine
4 ounces pork, shredded

1 tablespoon sherry
1 tablespoon light soy sauce
1 teaspoon sugar
2 ounces preserved Yunnan
    cabbage, julienne
1 large piece of aluminum foil

1. Rub cleaned chicken with salt. Rub ginger juice inside chicken. Set aside.
2. Heat 2 tablespoons oil in wok. Stir-fry scallion. Add pork. Stir on high heat. Add sherry, soy sauce, and sugar. Remove to bowl.
3. Heat 2 tablespoons oil in wok. Stir-fry cabbage. Pour in meat mixture. Stir-fry 1 minute (add more sugar if desired).
4. Stuff meat mixture into chicken. Wrap in foil and place in pan.
5. Preheat oven to 350 degrees. Bake chicken 1 hour. Then turn heat to 400 degrees and bake 15 more minutes.
6. Remove foil. Remove stuffing from chicken to platter. Cut chicken into bite-sized pieces. Arrange on top of stuffing. Serve hot.

May be prepared in advance through step 4, or frozen after step 5.

Serves 4 to 6

Chicken with Bean Sprouts   SHANGHAI

This is a delicate dish, crunchy and colorful. The chicken and bean sprouts are a remarkable complement to one another: the flavor of this savory recipe will surprise you.

1 pound chicken breasts, boned and skinned, julienne	**2 to 4 cups oil for deep-frying**
1½ teaspoons salt	**½ red pepper, julienne**
1 egg white	**½ green pepper, julienne**
1 tablespoon cornstarch	**½ pound bean sprouts, heads and ends nipped off**
	1 teaspoon chili paste with garlic

1. Put chicken in bowl. Add 1 teaspoon of salt, egg white, and cornstarch. Mix well with hand. Set aside.
2. Heat oil to 350 degrees in wok. Drop in chicken and deep-fry, stirring well until it separates. Drain.
3. Reheat 2 tablespoons of oil in clean wok. Stir-fry peppers and bean sprouts about 1 minute.
4. Pour chicken into wok. Add ½ teaspoon salt and chili paste. Stir-fry quickly until all ingredients are thoroughly heated. Serve hot.

May be prepared in advance through step 1. Do not freeze.

Serves 4 to 6

Gold home, silver home—they cannot compare with a simple happy home.

Chicken with Chestnuts   SHANGHAI

This is a well-known dish in Shanghai. With very little effort, the result is an outstanding family dinner.

1 pound fresh chestnuts*
4 tablespoons oil
1 slice ginger, ⅛ inch thick
1 stalk scallion, cut into 4 pieces
1 3-pound fryer, cut into
    2-inch pieces

2 tablespoons sherry
½ teaspoon salt
¼ cup dark soy sauce
2 cups water
1 tablespoon sugar

1. Cut chestnuts into halves. Cover with water. Simmer 30 minutes. Remove shells and skin. Set aside.
2. Heat oil in wok. Stir-fry ginger and scallion 30 seconds. Add chicken. Stir-fry 1 minute. Add sherry, salt, soy sauce, and water. Cover and simmer 30 minutes.
3. Add chestnuts and sugar. Simmer 10 minutes more.
4. Bring to high heat and cook 5 minutes. Remove to platter. Serve hot.

---

* Dried chestnuts may be used (soak in cold water overnight).

May be prepared in advance through step 3, or frozen after step 4.

Serves 4 to 6

Chicken with Chinese Greens and Ham   PEKING

This is a colorful and delicate chicken dish. It is also low in calories.

Boiling water
½ pound bok choy (Chinese
    green), cut into 1½-inch
    lengths
1 pound boneless and skinless
    chicken breast (preferably
    partially frozen), cut into thin
    slices
1½ teaspoons salt
1 tablespoon cornstarch
1 egg white
2 to 4 cups oil for deep-frying

4 slices bamboo shoots,
    cut same size as chicken
1 tablespoon sherry
¼ cup chicken stock
1 teaspoon cornstarch,
    dissolved in 2 teaspoons water
4 slices (cooked) Virginia ham,
    cut same size as chicken

1. Pour boiling water over bok choy. Boil 30 seconds. Drain. Rinse in cold water to retain green color. Set aside.
2. Combine chicken with ½ teaspoon of salt, cornstarch, and egg white. Mix well with hand.
3. Heat oil to moderate. Deep-fry chicken. Quickly drain. Remove to plate.
4. Reheat 2 tablespoons oil in wok. Stir-fry bamboo shoots and bok choy 2 minutes. Add chicken. Pour in sherry. Add 1 teaspoon salt. Pour in stock. Thicken with dissolved cornstarch. Garnish with ham slices. Serve hot.

May be prepared in advance through step 3. Do not freeze.

Serves 4 to 6

Chicken with Fermented Salted Black Beans   CANTON

The fermented black bean, which has a pungent flavor, is found mostly in Cantonese cooking.

1 2½-pound fryer, cut into
    1½-inch pieces
½ teaspoon salt
2 tablespoons dark soy sauce
1 teaspoon ginger juice
    (use garlic press)
1 egg white
1 tablespoon cornstarch

2 to 4 cups oil for deep-frying
1 clove garlic
2 tablespoons fermented
    black beans
1 tablespoon water
1 tablespoon sherry
1 cup chicken stock
½ cup pearl onions
¼ teaspoon sugar

1. Combine chicken with salt, 1 tablespoon of soy sauce, ginger juice, egg white, and cornstarch. Mix well with hand.
2. Heat oil to 375 degrees in wok. Deep-fry chicken 1 minute. Drain. Remove.
3. Pound garlic and 1 tablespoon of black beans with back of cleaver. Put into small bowl. Add 1 tablespoon water. Mix well. Set aside.
4. Reheat 2 tablespoons of oil in wok. Sauté garlic and black beans 1 minute. Pour in chicken. Stir-fry 5 seconds. Add sherry and 1 tablespoon soy sauce. Pour in stock. Cover and cook over moderate heat 10 minutes. Remove to large bowl.
5. Reheat 2 tablespoons oil in wok. Stir-fry pearl onions with 1 tablespoon black bean mixture 1 minute.
6. Add chicken. Cook 5 minutes over moderate heat. Add sugar. Bring to high heat. Stir-fry 1 minute. Serve hot.

May be prepared in advance through step 5, or frozen after step 6.

Serves 4 to 6

Chicken with Five Shreds   SZECHWAN

This is one of my original dishes that I love. The bean curd, which has no flavor, becomes well-flavored by the accompanying ingredients.

Sauce:

2 tablespoons light soy sauce
2 teaspoons sugar
1 tablespoon chili paste with garlic
1 tablespoon sherry
¼ cup chicken stock
1 teaspoon cornstarch

1 pound chicken breast, boned
    and skinned, julienne
1 teaspoon salt
1 egg white
1 tablespoon cornstarch
2 to 4 cups oil for deep-frying

2 cloves garlic, chopped fine
1 thin piece of ginger, julienne
1 scallion, julienne
¼ cup carrots, 1 inch in length,
    julienne
¼ red pepper, julienne
¼ green pepper, julienne
¼ cup bamboo shoots, julienne
4 dried black mushrooms, soaked
    in boiling water 20 minutes,
    cooked 20 minutes, stems
    removed, julienne
4 pieces white pressed bean curd,
    julienne

1. Combine sauce ingredients in a bowl. Set aside.
2. Combine chicken shreds with salt, egg white, and cornstarch. Mix lightly with hand.
3. Heat oil to 375 degrees in wok. Add chicken. Stir to separate (about 30 seconds). Drain. Set aside.
4. Reheat 2 tablespoons of oil in wok. Stir-fry garlic, ginger, and scallion 30 seconds. Add carrots, peppers, bamboo shoots, and mushrooms. Stir-fry over high heat 1 minute. Remove to bowl.
5. Reheat 2 tablespoons oil in wok. Add bean curd. Stir-fry over high heat 1 minute. Add all vegetables. Add chicken. Stir-fry again 3 minutes. Pour in sauce mixture. Stir-fry over brisk heat 2 minutes more. Serve hot.

May be prepared in advance through step 3, or frozen after step 4.

Serves 4 to 6

Chicken with Orange Peel   SZECHWAN

This is a delightful Szechwan dish. The combination of ingredients will surely please you.

1 2-pound fryer or 2 chicken
    breasts, boned and skinned,
    cut into 1-inch pieces
¼ teaspoon salt
2 tablespoons dark soy sauce
1 tablespoon cornstarch
4 cups oil for deep-frying
2 tablespoons sesame seed oil
2 tablespoons preserved orange
    peel or fresh dried orange
    rind,* cut into chunks

1 tablespoon scallion,
    chopped fine
1 tablespoon ginger, chopped fine
2 whole dried red chili peppers,
    cut into quarters
4½ teaspoons sherry
1 teaspoon red wine vinegar
¾ tablespoon sugar

1. Sprinkle chicken with salt. Mix with 1 tablespoon of soy sauce and cornstarch.
2. Heat oil to boiling. Deep-fry chicken 1 minute. Drain. Remove chicken and oil.
3. Heat sesame seed oil in wok. Stir-fry orange peel, scallion, ginger, and chili peppers 1 minute. Add sherry, 1 tablespoon soy sauce, wine vinegar, and sugar. Then add chicken. Stir-fry 2 minutes. Remove to platter. Serve hot.

---

* Put orange rind into 250-degree oven 1 hour or more, until dried.

May be prepared in advance. May be frozen.

Serves 4 to 6

One must be available, alert, active, and adaptable.

Chicken with Pine Nuts   YANGCHOW

This dish is superb. It is the most elegant Imperial dish.

1 pound chicken breast, boneless, skinless (partially frozen)
1 teaspoon salt
1 tablespoon cornstarch
2 egg whites
2 to 4 cups oil for deep-frying
⅓ cup pine nuts
1 scallion (white part only), chopped fine
½ clove garlic, chopped fine

¼ cup cooked Virginia ham, minced
¼ cup frozen peas, blanched in boiling water 1 minute and rinsed in cold water
Sauce:

2 tablespoons chicken stock
1 tablespoon sherry
½ teaspoon salt
½ teaspoon cornstarch

1. Cut chicken lengthwise ⅛-inch thick. Shred into thin slices. Then mince crosswise. Put into bowl.
2. Add salt, cornstarch, and egg whites. Mix thoroughly with hand. Set aside.
3. Thoroughly combine sauce ingredients in a bowl. Set aside.
4. Heat oil in wok. When it is warm, pour in chicken. Deep-fry chicken, stirring to separate, until it turns white. Remove by draining through strainer. Set aside.
5. Reheat oil. In strainer, deep-fry pine nuts until they are light brown, watching carefully not to burn. Drain nuts and set aside.
6. Reheat 1 tablespoon of oil in wok. Stir-fry scallion and garlic on low flame 30 seconds. Pour in sauce. Turn heat to high. Add chicken, ham, and peas. Toss quickly and cook briskly 1 minute. Remove to platter.
7. Sprinkle pine nuts over chicken. Serve hot.

May be prepared in advance through step 2. Do not freeze.

Serves 4 to 6

Chicken Salad with Rice Sticks   CANTON

You will love this version of chicken salad. It is delicious with beef and oyster sauce.

4 ounces rice sticks (Py Mai Fun)
2 to 4 cups oil for deep-frying
1 chicken breast or 2-pound fryer*
½ teaspoon salt
2 tablespoons light soy sauce
1 head lettuce, shredded
preserved red ginger, chopped

Sauce:

½ cup oil
¼ teaspoon salt
2 teaspoons sugar
½ cup red wine vinegar
½ cup light soy sauce
2 scallions, chopped fine
1 teaspoon pepper oil (optional)

1. Deep-fry rice sticks quickly, a few at a time in very hot oil until they puff, about 1 second. Drain. Remove.
2. Rub chicken with salt and soy sauce. Place in shallow pan. Pour 1 tablespoon of heated oil over chicken. Roast 45 minutes in 350-degree oven.
3. When chicken is cool, discard skin and bones and break meat apart with hands into shreds. Do not cut.
4. Combine first 5 ingredients of sauce in serving bowl. Mix well. Add scallions and pepper oil (this will make sauce spicy).
5. Add lettuce and chicken. Toss well. Arrange rice sticks on top. Garnish with preserved red ginger. Serve cold.

---

* You may substitute crab, lobster, shrimp, or barbecued pork for chicken.

May be prepared in advance through step 4. Only cooked chicken may be frozen.

Serves 4 to 6

Chicken Steamed with Chinese Sausage   CANTON

This is a simple recipe, so easy to make. The sausage gives a marvelous, sweet flavor that is wonderful combined with the chicken.

1 3-pound fryer,
    cut into 1½-inch pieces
½ teaspoon salt
½ teaspoon pepper
3 tablespoons dark soy sauce
1 tablespoon sherry
2 slices ginger, about ⅛-inch thick

1 stalk scallion
4 dried black mushrooms, soaked
    in boiling water 20 minutes,
    stems removed, cut into
    quarters
4 Chinese sausages, cut into
    ¼-inch diagonal slices

1. Put chicken into bowl. Sprinkle with salt and pepper. Add remaining ingredients.
2. Place bowl on rack in pot or in steamer. Cover and steam over boiling water 1 hour.

May be prepared in advance. May be frozen. Resteam before serving.

Serves 4 to 6

Never add soy sauce after serving. Have you ever seen an artist hang a picture on the wall and then take a brush and add strokes of paint?

Chicken with Sweet Corn   PEKING

This is a genuine banquet dish, delicate yet simple to prepare.

½ pound boneless and skinless
    chicken breast*
1 tablespoon cornstarch
1 teaspoon salt
4½ cups chicken stock
1 can sweet creamed corn

2 tablespoons cornstarch,
    dissolved in ¼ cup water
2 egg whites, beaten to soft peaks
Salt to taste
1 tablespoon sherry
2 tablespoons (cooked) Virginia
    ham, minced

1. Remove all tendons and sinew from chicken. Mince chicken very fine.
2. Add cornstarch, salt, and ½ cup of stock. Beat well in bowl or blender.
3. Bring 4 cups stock to boil. Add corn. Then add prepared chicken mixture. Bring to boil again. Thicken with dissolved cornstarch. Stir in beaten egg whites. Season to taste with salt. Add sherry.
4. Pour mixture into deep serving bowl. Garnish with minced ham on top.

---

   * One cup of crab meat may be substituted for chicken. When serving, add a pinch of pepper.

May be prepared in advance through step 2. Do not freeze.

Serves 4 to 6

Chicken Velvet PEKING

Basically delicate and dainty, this is an appealing dish with many flavors and textures.

2 chicken breasts,	**2 ounces pea pods (snow peas),**
boned and skinned	**strings removed**
1½ cups cold chicken stock	**1 tablespoon cornstarch,**
1½ teaspoons salt	**dissolved in 2 tablespoons**
2 tablespoons cornstarch	**water**
3 egg whites, beaten slightly stiff	**2 tablespoons (cooked) Virginia**
4 cups oil for deep-frying	**ham, minced**

1. Chop chicken very fine or grind in blender. Soak in ½ cup of cold stock.
2. Add 1 teaspoon of salt and 1 tablespoon of cornstarch to chicken. Mix well.
3. Fold beaten egg whites into chicken mixture. Mix 1 tablespoon cornstarch into chicken mixture, folding lightly.
4. Heat oil and deep-fry chicken mixture. Stir quickly with chopsticks in order to separate. Remove to plate. Drain oil.
5. Reheat 2 tablespoons of oil in wok. Over moderately high heat, stir-fry pea pods 30 seconds. Remove and set aside.
6. Reheat 2 tablespoons oil in wok. Add 1 cup stock. Season with ½ teaspoon salt. Put in chicken. Bring to boil. Thicken with dissolved cornstarch.
7. Serve on platter. Trim with pea pods. Garnish with minced ham on top.

May be prepared in advance through step 2. Do not freeze.

Serves 4 to 6

Chicken with Walnuts   PEKING

After 40 years of teaching, I must say that this dish reigns supreme. Food writers from England, Australia, and Germany have raved about it. My personal chef taught me how to make this dish in 1936. I know you, too, will love it.

1 3-pound fryer, boned, or 2
    chicken breasts, boned
    and skinned
1 teaspoon salt
1 egg white
1 tablespoon cornstarch
2 to 4 cups oil for deep-frying
1 cup walnut halves

1 red bell pepper, cut into
    ½-inch cubes
1 green pepper, cut into
    ½-inch cubes
2 tablespoons bean sauce
2 tablespoons sugar
¼ cup chicken stock
1 tablespoon sherry

1. Cut chicken into ½-inch cubes. Add salt, egg white, and cornstarch. Mix thoroughly with hand.
2. Deep-fry chicken in deep hot oil 2 minutes. Remove and drain.
3. In same oil over low heat, deep-fry walnuts in strainer until golden brown. Set aside. Drain oil.
4. Reheat 2 tablespoons oil in wok. Stir-fry red and green peppers 1 minute. Remove.
5. Reheat 2 tablespoons oil in wok. Add bean sauce. Stir 3 minutes. Lower heat. Add sugar. Stir 30 seconds, then add stock and sherry. Stir until dark brown.
6. Turn up heat. Pour in chicken and peppers. Stir-fry quickly 1 minute. Remove to platter.
7. Sprinkle fried walnuts over chicken and serve.

May be prepared in advance through step 5. Do not freeze.

Serves 4 to 6

Always taste every dish for flavor. Like an artist you are never finished until that last stroke of the brush.

Chicken Wings with Oyster Sauce   CANTON

The Chinese have many varied ways of cooking chicken wings. Here is an economical, simple-to-prepare dish with an exciting flavor.

12 chicken wings	**1 clove garlic, minced fine**
1½ tablespoons dark soy	**1 tablespoon sherry**
sauce	**1 cup water**
½ pound broccoli	**2 tablespoons oyster sauce**
½ teaspoon salt	**1 teaspoon sugar**
1½ tablespoons sesame seed	**1 teaspoon cornstarch**
oil	**dissolved in 1 teaspoon water**
2 to 4 cups oil for deep-frying	
1 scallion, cut into 2-inch lengths	
1 slice ginger, cut thin	

1. Divide each chicken wing into two pieces. Discard ends. Marinate in soy sauce 10 minutes. Coat evenly. Set aside.
2. Break broccoli into flowerets, cutting stems into 2-inch lengths. Blanch in boiling water 1 minute. Rinse with cold water. Drain. Sprinkle with salt and 1 tablespoon of sesame seed oil. Set aside.
3. Heat oil to 375 degrees in wok. Deep-fry chicken wings until golden brown. Drain. Set aside.
4. Reheat 1 tablespoon of oil. Stir-fry scallion, ginger, and garlic until there is an aroma, about 30 seconds. Add chicken wings, sherry, and water. Bring to boil. Cover and cook over moderate heat 15 minutes.
5. Add oyster sauce, sugar, and ½ tablespoon sesame seed oil. Stir-fry 15 seconds. Thicken with dissolved cornstarch.
6. Spoon wings onto platter. Arrange broccoli around them.

May be prepared in advance, or frozen after step 5.

Serves 6

Chungking Chicken   SZECHWAN

The following variation on chicken is very popular. It is subtle and spicy and is another of my favorites.

1 1-pound chicken breast, boned,   *Sauce:*
   skinned, cut into ½-inch cubes
1 egg white   **1 teaspoon sherry**
1 tablespoon light soy sauce   **1 tablespoon dark soy sauce**
1 teaspoon sherry   **2 teaspoons sugar**
1 tablespoon cornstarch   **1 teaspoon sesame seed oil**
4 cups oil for deep-frying   **1 teaspoon red wine vinegar**
1 tablespoon ginger, chopped fine   **1 teaspoon cornstarch**
1 scallion, chopped fine   **Pepper to taste**
2 cloves garlic, chopped fine
1 tablespoon chili paste with garlic

1. Combine chicken with egg white, soy sauce, sherry, and cornstarch. Mix well with hand. Set aside.
2. Blend sauce ingredients in small bowl. Set aside.
3. Heat oil to 350 degrees in wok. Deep-fry chicken about 45 seconds. Remove by draining through strainer.
4. Reheat 1 tablespoon of oil in wok. Add ginger, scallion, garlic, and chili paste with garlic. Stir-fry until aroma comes, about 30 seconds. Pour in chicken. Stir-fry on brisk heat 1 minute. Pour in sauce mixture. Stir-fry over high heat 10 more seconds.

May be prepared in advance through step 2, or frozen after step 4.

Serves 4 to 6

Drunken Chicken   SHANGHAI

This is an easy way to make Drunken Chicken.   It is marinated in wine—making it exotic and exciting.   It's said that the Chinese do not get drunk because they are in the habit of cooking so many foods with wine.

2 cups water
1 chicken breast
2 slices ginger, ⅛-inch thick
1 scallion

1 tablespoon salt
½ cup sherry
Chinese parsley (Celantro)
    for garnish

1. Bring water to boil.
2. Add chicken breast, ginger, scallion, and salt. Boil 15 minutes.
3. Remove to bowl. Bone chicken while warm. Remove ginger and scallion and discard.
4. Place chicken and its stock in container. Add sherry. Cover and refrigerate 1 to 5 days.
5. When ready to serve, cut chicken into 1-inch pieces. Arrange on platter.
6. Pour jellied liquid over chicken and decorate with parsley. Serve cold.

May be prepared in advance. Do not freeze.

Serves 4 to 6

Food enlivens the spirit and enthusiasm for people.

Empress Chicken   YANGCHOW

During the Ching dynasty, Emperor Chien Lung used to tour different cities. He was served this dish for dinner at a well-known restaurant in Yangchow, which was known for its outstanding chefs. His Empress enjoyed it so much she expressed a desire to know what it was called. The chef cleverly replied, "This is called 'Empress Chicken.'"

1 3-pound fryer
2 tablespoons flour
2 tablespoons light soy sauce
4 tablespoons oil
½ pound leeks, washed and cut
    into 1½-inch pieces
4 dried black mushrooms, soaked
    in boiling water 20 minutes,
    stems removed

4 pieces of Virginia ham, cut
    into ⅛-inch pieces
1 tablespoon Worcestershire
    sauce
1 tablespoon sherry
1 teaspoon salt
½ teaspoon sugar

1. Chop chicken into 2-inch pieces. Mix with flour and soy sauce.
2. Heat 2 tablespoons of oil in wok and stir-fry chicken until light brown. Remove and drain. Set aside.
3. Heat 2 tablespoons oil in wok. Stir-fry leeks over medium heat until light brown.
4. Put leeks into a flameproof casserole dish. Add chicken. Pour in water to half cover. Bring to boil. Simmer 30 minutes.
5. Add mushrooms, ham, Worcestershire sauce, sherry, salt and sugar.
6. Cook 10 minutes over medium heat. Baste occasionally. Serve in casserole.

May be prepared in advance. May be frozen. Reheat before serving.

Serves 4 to 6

Fried Eight Pieces

This dish may be used as an hors d'oeuvre or an entrée. It is delicious hot or cold.

1 3-pound fryer
½ teaspoon salt
¼ teaspoon pepper
2 tablespoons dark soy sauce
1 tablespoon sherry

½ teaspoon garlic juice (use garlic press)
1 egg white
3 tablespoons cornstarch
4 cups oil for deep-frying
Peppercorn salt

1. Cut chicken into 1½-inch pieces. Season with salt and pepper.
2. Marinate chicken in soy sauce, sherry, and garlic juice 1 hour, turning occasionally.
3. Remove chicken and mix it with egg white and cornstarch.
4. Heat oil to 375 degrees in wok. Deep-fry chicken 5 minutes and lift out in strainer.
5. Reheat oil. Deep-fry again 1 minute (this makes chicken crispy). Drain.
6. Serve with peppercorn salt.

May be prepared in advance through step 2, or frozen after step 5. Refry before serving.

Serves 4 to 6

I am afraid that I am deeply in love with food as my companion, my non-failing pal, my lifelong chum.

Jade Chicken   CANTON

The stories circulated about the Dowager Empress of the Ching dynasty have flabbergasted people. The pomp and luxury of her court were unbelievable: a light meal consisted of 40 courses; dinner usually had 100. The Empress was very fussy. Her chef was always trying to please her palate. This recipe, in which he had to peel grapes, was one of her favorites.

½ pound Ribier grapes
1 3-pound fryer or
    2 chicken breasts, cut into
    2-inch pieces
1 teaspoon salt
1 tablespoon light soy sauce
4 tablespoons oil

2 tablespoons fermented
    black beans
1 tablespoon water
1 cup onions, diced
1 tablespoon sherry
1 cup water
1 tablespoon sugar

1. Remove skin from grapes. Set aside.
2. Mix chicken with salt and soy sauce.
3. Heat 2 tablespoons of oil in wok. Stir-fry chicken until light brown. Remove.
4. Pound fermented black beans until they become pasty. Add 1 tablespoon water. Mix well. Set aside.
5. Heat 2 tablespoons of oil in wok and sauté onions. Add black bean paste. Stir-fry until aroma of beans comes out, about 1 minute. Put chicken into this sauce. Add sherry and water. Bring to boil. Cover and simmer 30 minutes.
6. Bring to high heat. Add sugar. Baste chicken with liquid 1 minute. Remove chicken to platter.
7. Add grapes to liquid. Bring to boil 1 minute. Pour mixture over chicken.

May be prepared in advance, or frozen after step 6.

Serves 4 to 6

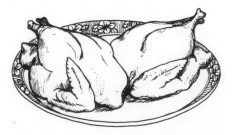

Kung Pao Chicken
(Spiced)

SZECHWAN

A great many Chinese dishes have historical backgrounds and origins. This dish bears the name of a high-ranking officer who died during the Ching dynasty. It is a very popular dish of the Szechwan school.

2 whole chicken breasts, boned,
    skinned, cut into ½-inch cubes
½ teaspoon salt
1 egg white
1 tablespoon cornstarch
2 cups oil for deep-frying
½ cup skinless roasted peanuts
10 whole dried red chili peppers
2 scallions, cut into
    ½-inch lengths
2 cloves garlic, minced

Sauce:

1 teaspoon chili paste with garlic
2 tablespoons dark soy sauce
1 tablespoon sherry
1 teaspoon red wine vinegar
1 teaspoon sugar
¼ cup chicken stock
1 teaspoon cornstarch
1 teaspoon sesame seed oil

1. Combine chicken, salt, egg white, and cornstarch. Mix well with hand. Set aside.
2. In a small bowl, blend sauce ingredients. Set aside.
3. Heat oil to 350 degrees in wok. Deep-fry chicken until it separates and is almost cooked. Remove by draining through strainer.
4. Reheat same oil. Deep-fry peanuts in strainer over moderate heat until they are golden brown. Remove by draining through strainer.
5. Reheat 2 tablespoons of oil in wok to smoking hot. Stir-fry red chili peppers until they are dark red. Lower heat. Add scallions and garlic. Stir-fry 30 seconds.
6. Pour in chicken. Stir-fry on high heat 1 minute.
7. Add sauce. Stir-fry until thoroughly heated and glazed. Add peanuts.

May be prepared in advance through step 4. Do not freeze.

Serves 4 to 6

Lemon Chicken   ALL REGIONS

This is an extremely popular dish, with many versions. This is my original version. It is easy to prepare. Just be sure to remember that the batter should resemble runny pancake batter and that the lemon sauce should have the consistency of maple syrup.

2 whole chicken breasts, boned and skinned	**½ cup sugar**
1 teaspoon salt	**1 cup sweet rice flour**
½ teaspoon pepper	**Cold water**
4 tablespoons flour	**Pinch of salt and pepper**
4 lemons	**4 cups oil for deep-frying**
1 cup water	**3 tablespoons cornstarch, dissolved in 6 tablespoons water**
	1 egg yolk

1. Trim fat from chicken. Cut each breast into 4 long pieces. Remove tendons. Season chicken with salt and pepper. Dredge each piece with flour. Set aside.
2. Finely grate rind from 2 lemons. Squeeze juice from them. (Slice 2 other lemons for garnish.)
3. Mix lemon juice with water, sugar, and grated rind. Set aside.
4. For batter: Mix 1 cup sweet rice flour with cold water (should be a little runny). Add a pinch of salt and pepper.
5. Heat oil to 375 degrees in wok. Dip chicken into batter. Deep-fry until light golden brown. Drain. Put on serving platter. Keep warm.
6. Heat lemon mixture. Thicken with dissolved cornstarch. Beat egg yolk. Add to lemon mixture, stirring rapidly until completely combined. (Be very careful to do this quickly or egg will curdle in the sauce. To be safe, add a few tablespoons hot sauce to beaten egg yolk to heat it up. Then add egg to remaining sauce, combining completely.)
7. Cut chicken into bite-sized pieces and serve with lemon sauce. Garnish with lemon slices.

May be prepared in advance through step 5. Refry before serving. Do not freeze.

Serves 4 to 6

Lychee Chicken with Sweet, Sour Sauce   CANTON

This is a delicious, versatile entrée. Shrimp, fish, or pork may be substituted for the chicken, and pineapple chunks may be used in place of the lychees.

**1 pound chicken fillet, cut into
    1-inch pieces**
1 teaspoon salt
1 egg
6 tablespoons cornstarch
2 to 4 cups oil for deep-frying

Sauce:

6 tablespoons tomato catsup
6 tablespoons white vinegar
6 tablespoons sugar
1½ cups cold water
**3 tablespoons cornstarch,
    dissolved in 3 tablespoons
    water**
½ onion, cut into ½-inch cubes
½ red pepper, cut into ½-inch cubes
**½ green pepper, cut into ½-inch
    cubes**
16 to 20 lychees

1. Combine chicken with salt, egg, and cornstarch. Mix well with hand.
2. Heat oil to smoking hot. Drop chicken into oil one piece at a time. Deep-fry until crispy (about 3 minutes). Remove chicken and set aside.
3. To make sauce: Put catsup, vinegar, sugar, and water into saucepan. Bring to boil. Stir in dissolved cornstarch. Add onion, peppers, and lychees at the last minute.
4. Reheat deep oil until it is almost smoking. Fry chicken 1 minute more, separating the pieces. Remove to platter. Pour sauce over chicken. Serve hot.

May be prepared in advance through step 2. Do not freeze.

Serves 4 to 6

Odd Flavor Chicken Salad   SZECHWAN

Nuts and fried rice sticks may also be added to this tempting dish that is a refreshing change to an American standby.

¼ cup dark soy sauce
2 tablespoons honey
1 clove garlic, minced
1 3-pound chicken
4 cups boiling water
2 tablespoons oil
2 scallions, chopped fine

1 slice ginger ⅛-inch thick,
  chopped fine
½ teaspoon red pepper flakes
½ teaspoon chili paste with
  garlic
1 teaspoon peppercorn salt
1 head lettuce, shredded

1. Combine soy sauce, honey, and garlic. Let stand 5 minutes.
2. Place whole chicken in boiling water. Boil 15 minutes. Turn off heat. Let chicken stand in water 20 minutes more. Cool. Bone and shred.
3. Heat oil in wok. Add scallions, ginger, red pepper flakes, chili paste with garlic, and peppercorn salt. Stir-fry 30 seconds. Cool.
4. Add sauce to scallion mixture. Stir thoroughly.
5. Combine shredded chicken with shredded lettuce in bowl. Pour sauce over this mixture. Toss thoroughly. Serve cold.

May be prepared in advance through step 4. Toss before serving. Do not freeze.

Serves 4 to 6

If you have many best friends, you have no friends.

Chicken, Peking Style

This is a succulent dish that I cook whenever I entertain. The sauce makes it outstanding.

1 2½-pound fryer or
    2 whole breasts, boned
2 teaspoons salt
Pinch of pepper
1 egg
6 tablespoons flour
1 tablespoon sherry
2 to 4 cups oil for deep-frying
2 tablespoons Chinese parsley
    (Celantro), chopped fine

Sauce:

1 tablespoon ginger, chopped fine
1 scallion, chopped fine
1 large garlic clove, chopped fine
1 cup chicken stock

1. Cut chicken into four pieces. Rub with salt and pepper.
2. Beat egg lightly. Stir in flour and mix into a paste. Add sherry. This forms batter.
3. Put chicken into batter until evenly coated. Mix well.
4. Heat oil to 375 degrees in wok. Turn to medium heat. Deep-fry chicken 5 minutes. Drain. Set aside.
5. To make sauce: Reheat 2 tablespoons oil in wok. Sauté ginger, scallion, and garlic 1 second. Pour in stock. Season to taste.
6. Add chicken to sauce. Boil 3 minutes. Add parsley. Boil 1 second.
7. When ready to serve, remove chicken and cut into small portions. Reheat sauce. Arrange pieces on a platter and pour sauce over.

May be prepared in advance, or frozen after step 4.

Serves 4 to 6

Smoked Chicken   PEKING

A little time-consuming, but oh, so delicious!

1 3-pound fryer	1 tablespoon light soy sauce
2 teaspoons salt	2 tablespoons black tea
Juice from 1 slice ginger (use garlic press)	2 tablespoons brown sugar
1 tablespoon sherry	2 tablespoons uncooked long-grain rice
1 stalk scallion	1 tablespoon sesame seed oil

1. Rub chicken with salt inside and out. Pour ginger juice inside. Add sherry and scallion.
2. Place chicken in bowl on rack in pot or in steamer. Cover and steam over boiling water 35 minutes. Cool.
3. Rub chicken with soy sauce.
4. Line inside of wok with aluminum foil (line cover also). Put black tea, brown sugar, and rice on the foil. Place a greased rack in wok. Put chicken on rack. Bring to high heat.
5. Cover wok tightly (this prevents smoke from escaping).
6. Smoke chicken 10 minutes, turning after 5 minutes. Brown both sides evenly. Smoke 5 minutes more.
7. Remove chicken. Brush with sesame seed oil. Cut into bite-sized pieces before serving. Serve hot or cold.

May be prepared in advance, or frozen after step 6.

Serves 4 to 6

Crispy Chicken Legs   PEKING

A delicious snack or hors d' oeuvre that is also lovely on a buffet table.

6 chicken drumsticks	1 tablespoon light soy sauce
1½ teaspoons salt	2 tablespoons cornstarch
1 tablespoon sherry	4 cups oil for deep-frying
1 thin slice ginger	1 tablespoon peppercorn salt
1 stalk scallion	

1. Rub chicken thoroughly with salt. Put into oven-proof bowl. Marinate 2 hours in sherry, ginger, and scallion mixture.

2. Place bowl containing chicken and marinade on rack in pot or in steamer. Cover and steam over boiling water 30 minutes.
3. Rub drumsticks with soy sauce. Sprinkle heavily with cornstarch.
4. Deep-fry in heated oil 3 minutes or until crispy.
5. Serve hot or cold with peppercorn salt.

May be prepared in advance through step 3, or frozen after step 4. If frozen, thaw and refry before serving.

Serves 4 to 6

Thousand-Year-Sauce Chicken   ALL REGIONS

This master marinade can be kept indefinitely in the refrigerator so that you can use it every time you prepare this recipe. Each restaurant in China has its own version of it. Use the same sauce with chicken wings as an hors d' oeuvre.

1 stick cinnamon	**½ cup sherry**
2 anise seeds	**½ cup sesame seed oil**
1½ teaspoons fennel seeds	**1 3-pound frying chicken**
4 cups water	**2 tablespoons sugar**
1 cup dark soy sauce	

1. Put cinnamon stick, anise seeds, and fennel seeds into a cheesecloth bag. Tie it.
2. Pour water, soy sauce, sherry, and sesame seed oil into an earthenware pot or casserole. Bring to boil. Put bag into sauce mixture.
3. Put chicken into pot. Bring to boil. Simmer over low heat 45 minutes. Turn chicken 2 or 3 times during cooking. Cool in sauce about 5 minutes. Remove.
4. Cut chicken into bite-sized pieces before serving. To serve hot, heat ½ cup of sauce and pour over chicken; to serve cold, the sauce is not necessary.

NOTE: When reusing sauce, add proportionate soy sauce, sherry, and sesame seed oil to taste.

May be prepared in advance through step 4, or frozen after step 3.

Serves 4 to 6

Winter Garden Special   YANGCHOW

This sweet, sour, and spicy dish is served at the Winter Garden Restaurant in Los Angeles. Many students have requested the recipe. Here it is.

1 pound chicken breast, skinned, boned, cut into 1-inch cubes
1 egg, beaten
1½ teaspoons salt
1 tablespoon cornstarch
¼ cup flour
2 to 4 cups oil for deep-frying
1 scallion, chopped fine
1 pound fresh spinach, cleaned, stems removed

Sauce

¼ cup tomato catsup
1 teaspoon hot pepper oil
2 tablespoons sugar
¼ cup chicken stock
1 teaspoon cornstarch

1. Combine chicken, egg, 1 teaspoon of salt, and cornstarch. Mix well with hand. Coat chicken evenly with flour. Discard leftover flour. Set aside.
2. In a small bowl, blend sauce ingredients.
3. Heat oil to 375 degrees in wok. Deep-fry chicken a few pieces at a time until golden brown and crispy, about 2 minutes. Drain through strainer.
4. Reheat 2 tablespoons oil in wok. Add scallion. Stir-fry quickly. Pour in sauce. Heat to boiling point.
5. Add chicken. Stir-fry 30 seconds. Put on platter.
6. Reheat 3 tablespoons of oil in wok until smoking hot. Add ½ teaspoon salt. Stir-fry spinach briskly 1 minute. Discard liquid. Arrange spinach around chicken on platter.

May be prepared in advance through step 2. Do not freeze.

Serves 4 to 6

The best lovers make love on a full stomach.

Won Ton Supreme   SHANGHAI

There are endless creations for a chef. This is indeed a supreme one.

4 ounces fresh shrimp, shelled,
    deveined, cut into halves
    lengthwise
4 ounces chicken breast, boned,
    skinned, cut into thin slices
3 ounces flank steak, cut thin
    across the grain
2 ounces pork loin, cut thin
1 teaspoon salt
1 egg white
1 tablespoon cornstarch
½ pound broccoli
2 to 4 cups oil for deep-frying

10 pieces ready-made raw Won Ton
    (See Index)
6 pea pods (snow peas), strings
    removed
¼ cup bamboo shoots, cut into
    thin slices
Sauce:

2 tablespoons dark soy sauce
¼ cup chicken stock
1 tablespoon sherry
½ teaspoon sugar
1 teaspoon cornstarch

1. Mix shrimp, chicken, beef, and pork with salt, egg white, and cornstarch. Set aside.
2. Break broccoli into flowerets. Peel off woody part of stems. Slice stems diagonally into bite-sized pieces. Blanch broccoli in boiling water 1 minute. Rinse in cold water. Drain. Set aside.
3. In a small bowl, blend sauce ingredients. Set aside.
4. Heat oil to 375 degrees in wok. Deep-fry chicken mixture about 1 minute. Drain. Remove to plate.
5. Deep-fry won tons in same oil until golden brown. Drain and remove. Dry on paper towel.
6. Reheat 2 tablespoons of oil in clean wok. Add broccoli, pea pods, and bamboo shoots. Stir-fry 1 minute. Add chicken, meat, and shrimp mixture. Stir-fry over brisk fire 1 minute. Pour in sauce. Cook 1 minute more. Spoon mixture onto platter. Arrange won tons around platter.

May be prepared in advance through step 3, or frozen after step 4.

Serves 4 to 6

5

Duck and Squab

The Chinese are great lovers of duck and squab. So much so that the Chinese who lived in the United States during World War II did not feel the meat-rationing pinch.

The most famous of all ducks are from Peking. They are fragrant, have fine skin for roasting, and are beautiful to look at. In this country, too, you can buy excellent duck. Long Island ducklings are very good for roasted dishes. If you cannot get fresh duck, frozen ones are fine—just allow at least 10 hours to thaw at room temperature.

Crispy Duck   SZECHWAN

Crispy Duck is tender and juicy inside and crispy on the outside. It is so flavorful and easy to prepare—a culinary favorite that is delicious with pea pods and mushrooms. A steamer is necessary for this dish.

1 5-pound duck	2 tablespoons dark soy sauce
2 tablespoons salt	6 tablespoons flour
1 piece ginger ¼-inch thick	8 cups oil for deep-frying
1 scallion, cut into 4 pieces	2 tablespoons peppercorn salt

1. Wash duck and wipe dry. Rub with salt inside and out.
2. Put ginger and scallion inside duck. Set aside for at least 4 hours.
3. Place duck directly on steamer tray. Steam covered over boiling water 1½ to 2 hours. Remove. Set aside and cool.
4. Brush duck with soy sauce. Sprinkle flour on duck, rubbing well into skin and coating thoroughly.
5. When oil is very hot, fry duck until crispy and golden brown, turning occasionally.
6. Serve whole or cut into pieces with plum sauce. Plain steamed buns and peppercorn salt are a delicious accompaniment.

May be prepared in advance through step 5. Refry before serving. May be frozen after step 3.

Serves 4 to 6

Duck with Bean Sprouts   PEKING

This is a great way to make use of leftover duck.

4 tablespoons oil	½ teaspoon salt
2 cups roast duck, sliced thin,	1 teaspoon sugar
skin removed	2 tablespoons light soy sauce
1 pound bean sprouts	

1. Put 2 tablespoons of oil in heated wok. Lightly stir-fry duck slices 10 seconds. Remove and set aside.
2. Heat 2 tablespoons oil in wok. Stir-fry bean sprouts on brisk heat 1 minute. Add salt and sugar. Add in duck. Add soy sauce. Stir-fry 1 minute. Serve immediately.

May be prepared in advance through step 1. Do not freeze.

Serves 4 to 6

Duck with Leeks   SHANGHAI

*When saving time is important, you can prepare duck with leeks: it can be
made a day in advance and it is fail-proof.   Try it with Chinese Chicken
Salad.*

1 4-or 5-pound duck
1 teaspoon salt
3 tablespoons light soy sauce
4 tablespoons oil
2 tablespoons dry sherry

3 cups water
1 pound leeks, washed, cleaned,
   cut into 1½-inch pieces
1 tablespoon sugar
1½ tablespoons cornstarch,
   dissolved in 3 tablespoons
   water

1. Put duck in water to cover. Boil 2 minutes. Discard water. Place duck
in strainer to dry.
2. Rub duck with salt and 1 tablespoon of soy sauce. Fry whole duck in 2
tablespoons heated oil until light brown. Add sherry. Cover ¾ of duck
with water.
3. Add 2 tablespoons soy sauce. Cover and simmer until tender, about 1
hour.
4. Fry leeks in 2 tablespoons heated oil until light brown. Add leeks to
duck. Simmer 1 hour more.
5. Add sugar.   Bring to high heat.   Thicken liquid with dissolved
cornstarch. Serve duck hot in Chinese earthenware pot; if not available, use
casserole dish.

May be prepared in advance. May be frozen. Reheat before serving.

Serves 4 to 6

Chinese cooking is as representative of Chinese culture as poetry or
painting. It is an art with endless possibilities.

Duck with Onions   SHANGHAI

This recipe is simple but will always receive applause when served over rice.

1 4- to 5-pound duck
4 tablespoons dark soy sauce
4 tablespoons oil
1 thin slice ginger
1 whole scallion, quartered
1 tablespoon sherry
2½ cups water (to half cover duck)

1 pound onions (about 3), sliced
   thin
4 bamboo shoots, sliced thin
3 dried black mushrooms, soaked
   in boiling water 20 minutes,
   stems removed
1 tablespoon sugar

1. Rub duck with 1 tablespoon of soy sauce.
2. Heat 2 tablespoons oil in wok. Stir-fry ginger and scallion. Fry duck in same oil until light brown. Pour in sherry. Add 3 tablespoons soy sauce and water. Bring to boil. Simmer 1½ hours. Cool. Refrigerate duck with sauce overnight.
3. Remove to plate. Skim all fat from jellied sauce.
4. Heat remaining 2 tablespoons oil and stir-fry onions until soft and brown, about 20 minutes. Add duck and sauce to onions and simmer until duck is tender, about 30 minutes.
5. Add bamboo shoots and mushrooms. Cook 10 minutes.
6. Bring to high heat. Add sugar. Cook until sauce thickens. Serve hot or cold.

May be prepared in advance. May be frozen.

Serves 4 to 6

The impossible will always be possible.

Lacquered Duck   SOOCHOW

Lacquered Duck is red duck. (Red rice gives it the color.)

2 whole star anise	**Water**
1 cinnamon stick	**1 slice ginger**
2 tablespoons red rice	**1 stalk scallion**
(available in Chinese markets)	**2 tablespoons sherry**
1 5-pound duck	**2 tablespoons sugar**
2 tablespoons salt	

1. Put star anise, cinnamon stick, and red rice in cheesecloth. Tie it to make a spice bag. Set aside.
2. Wash duck and wipe dry. Rub with salt inside and out. Set aside 2 hours or refrigerate overnight.
3. Put duck in pot and cover ¾ with water. Add ginger, scallion, sherry, and spice bag. Bring to boil. Simmer about 2 hours.
4. Turn duck occasionally. Baste frequently to prevent burning. Duck should be evenly red.
5. Remove duck. Discard spice bag. Skim off fat from liquid. Add sugar and cook liquid over high heat until gravy thickens. Stir constantly until gravy is reduced to about ⅓ cup.
6. Cool duck. Cut into pieces. Put on platter. Pour gravy over duck. Serve cold.

May be prepared in advance. May be frozen.

Serves 4 to 6

Peking Duck   PEKING

The Peking Duck has traveled far and wide in reputation. It is a gourmet's delight and the following recipe is a sure and easy way to cook it.

1 5- to 6-pound duck	1 tablespoon white vinegar
8 cups water	1 tablespoon sherry
1 slice ginger	1½ tablespoons
1 scallion, cut into halves	cornstarch, dissolved in 3
3 tablespoons honey	tablespoons water
	Scallions for garnish

1. Clean duck. Wipe dry and tie string around neck.
2. Hang duck in cool, windy place 4 hours.
3. Fill large wok with water. Bring to boil. Add ginger, scallion, honey, vinegar, and sherry. Bring to boil. Pour in dissolved cornstarch. Stir constantly.

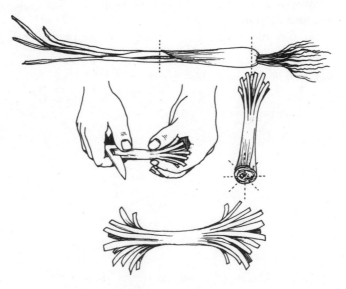

4. Place duck in large strainer above larger bowl. Scoop boiling mixture all over duck for about 10 minutes.

5. Hang duck again in cool, windy place for 6 hours until thoroughly dry.

6. Place duck breast side up on a greased rack in oven preheated to 350 degrees. Set a pan filled with 2 inches of water on bottom of oven. (This is for drippings.) Roast 30 minutes.

7. Turn duck and roast 30 minutes more.

8. Turn breast side up again. Roast 10 minutes more.

9. Use sharp knife to cut off crispy skin. Serve meat and skin immediately on a prewarmed dish.

10. The duck is eaten hot with hoisin sauce rolled in Chinese Pancakes (recipe follows). Garnish with scallion flowerets.

May be prepared in advance through step 5. Do not freeze.

Serves 4 to 6

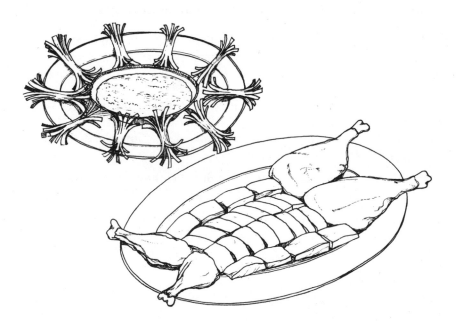

Chinese Pancakes   PEKING

These pancakes, served with Peking Duck, are also served with Moo Shu Pork or any shredded meat or vegetable. Adding hoisin sauce to the center of each pancake before filling makes them even more delicious.

1 cup flour   **2 tablespoons sesame seed oil**
½ cup boiling water   **Aluminum foil**

1. Put flour in bowl. Make a well. Add boiling water. Stir quickly with chopsticks or fork until water is absorbed and all flour comes away from side of bowl.
2. Knead dough on lightly floured board until smooth.
3. Put dough in bowl and cover with damp cloth. Let stand 20 minutes.
4. Return dough to floured board. Knead a little more. Make into long, sausage-like roll about 1½ inches in diameter.
5. Cut dough into 8 even pieces. Flatten each into a very thin round cake with palm.
6. Brush one side of each pancake evenly with a little sesame seed oil. Place one on another, oiled sides together, to form 4 stacks.
7. Roll each stack into a 7-inch circle.
8. Heat ungreased frying pan over medium heat. Cook pancake on both sides until it puffs up slightly. Do not brown.
9. Remove. Separate into 2 pancakes. Repeat until all are cooked and separated.
10. Put stack of pancakes in aluminum foil. Fold over the sides to keep cakes from drying out.
11. Place foil-wrapped pancakes in a steamer. Cover and steam over boiling water about 10 minutes.

NOTE: These pancakes can be kept frozen for months. It is a good idea to make a large quantity so they will be ready whenever you need them.

May be prepared in advance. Resteam before serving. May be frozen. If frozen, thaw out in foil and resteam in foil for 20 minutes.

8 pancakes

Pineapple and Duck CANTON

You will prize this recipe. The pineapple, ginger, and nut paste give a memorable flavor and the crab apple wafer adds a surprisingly lovely color.

1 small can sliced pineapple
1½ cups cooked duck, sliced
¼ cup preserved ginger slices
1 package dried crab apple
    wafers (or ½ cup jellied
    cranberry sauce)
½ cup hot chicken stock

¼ cup sesame seed paste
    (if not available, use peanut
    butter)
¼ cup cold chicken stock
¼ cup pineapple juice
1 teaspoon sugar
½ teaspoon salt

1. Cut each pineapple slice into 8 sections. Reserve ¼ cup juice.
2. In bowl, combine duck, pineapple, and ginger slices. Set aside.
3. Soak dried crab apple wafers in hot stock. Let cool. Stir well.
4. Mix sesame seed paste with cold stock. Add crab apple mixture, pineapple juice, sugar, and salt. Stir well.
5. Mix half of this sauce with duck mixture. Pour remaining sauce over it. Serve cold.

May be prepared in advance and refrigerated (covered) through step 4. Do not freeze.

Serves 4 to 6

Let my cooking stay in your heart.

Salted Duck   NANKING

This duck is a famous Nanking dish. It is served cold and is lovely on a buffet table.

1 5-pound duck	1 tablespoon ginger juice
2 tablespoons salt	(use garlic press)
	Water

1. Wash and clean duck. Wipe dry with paper towel.
2. Rub duck with salt inside and out. Wrap in foil. Refrigerate 3 days.
3. Rub inside of duck with ginger juice.
4. Put duck in large saucepan. Cover with water. Bring to boil. Simmer 2 hours.
5. Chill duck. Chop into bite-sized pieces. Serve cold.

May be prepared in advance. May be frozen.

Serves 4 to 6

Smoked Duck   HUNAN

This is the most succulent duck you have ever had. Once you try it, you will use it many times for buffets.

1 5-pound duck	½ cup brown sugar
2 tablespoons salt	1 tablespoon light soy sauce
1 tablespoon peppercorns	1 tablespoon cornstarch
Aluminum foil	4 cups oil for deep-frying
½ cup black tea leaves	Peppercorn salt
½ cup rice (uncooked)	

1. Clean and wash duck. Dry thoroughly with paper towel. Rub inside and out with salt. Sprinkle with peppercorns.
2. Wrap duck in aluminum foil and place a heavy weight on top. Refrigerate overnight.
3. Remove foil and place duck on steamer tray. Cover and steam over boiling water 1½ hours.
4. Line large wok and wok lid with aluminum foil. Place tea leaves, rice, and brown sugar on foil.

5. Put a rack above the mixture or place 4 chopsticks crosswise approximately 1 inch above it.

6. Place duck on rack, breast side up. Cover wok and seal tightly to prevent smoke from escaping.

7. Turn on high heat. Roast tea mixture until it smokes.

8. Smoke duck 10 minutes on high heat. Reduce heat to moderate. Smoke another 10 minutes. Turn off heat. Leave duck in wok 20 minutes more.

9. Remove duck. Cool thoroughly. Rub with soy sauce. Sprinkle evenly with cornstarch.

10. Heat oil in wok and deep-fry duck 10 minutes (5 minutes each side). Remove. Drain on paper towel.

11. Chop into bite-sized pieces. Serve hot with peppercorn salt and buns.

May be prepared in advance or frozen after step 10. Thaw and refry before serving.

Serves 4 to 6

Fried Squab   CANTON

Fried squab is a delicacy in China that is served at banquets. I believe it is an especially nutritious poultry because squabs eat finer grains than any other fowl.

2 1-pound squabs	**¼ cup dark soy sauce**
1 teaspoon salt	**1 tablespoon sherry**
⅛ teaspoon pepper	**1 teaspoon sugar**
1 stalk scallion, quartered	**2 to 4 cups oil for deep frying**
1 teaspoon ginger juice (use	**Peppercorn salt**
garlic press)	**Lemon wedges**

1. Clean squabs. Wipe dry. Rub with salt and pepper.

2. Put 2 pieces of scallion and half of ginger juice inside squabs. Rub other half ginger juice evenly on outside. Combine soy sauce, sherry, and sugar. Marinate squabs in this mixture for 1 hour. Drain. Discard marinade.

3. Heat oil in wok until smoking hot. Put in squabs. Turn to moderate heat. Deep-fry squabs 10 minutes, until golden brown. Drain.

4. Chop each squab into 8 pieces. Serve immediately with peppercorn salt and lemon wedges.

May be prepared in advance, or frozen after step 3, but step 3 must be repeated before serving.

Serves 4 to 6

Young Ginger With Duck Slices   CANTON

Ginger was used many years ago as an herb or as a cure for colds. Today it is a must in Chinese cooking. Note that young ginger has pink sprouts and a more tender skin than ginger root. A delectable dish, no one would suspect it uses leftover duck. It is delicious with Imperial Shrimp.

½ roast duck, sliced thin, skin
    removed
4 tablespoons oil
2 ounces young ginger, sliced thin
½ pound broccoli stalks, sliced thin
1 teaspoon salt

1 tablespoon bean or hoisin sauce
1 tablespoon sugar
1 tablespoon light soy sauce
1 tablespoon dry sherry
4 tablespoons chicken stock

1. Put 1 tablespoon oil in heated wok. When hot, stir-fry duck quickly for 30 seconds. Remove and set aside.
2. Heat 2 tablespoons of oil in wok. Add ginger, broccoli, and salt. Stir-fry 1 minute. Remove.
3. Heat 1 tablespoon oil and stir-fry bean or hoisin sauce. Add sugar, soy sauce, sherry, and stock.
4. Pour in broccoli mixture and duck. Stir-fry on high flame 10 seconds. Serve immediately.

May be prepared in advance through step 3, or frozen after step 4.

Serves 4 to 6

A good dish is like a successful marriage in which the parties involved are compatible and complement one another.

Minced Squab With Lettuce CANTON

This is a delicate banquet dish that is perfect for the calorie-conscious: lettuce leaves rather than bread make the "sandwich."

1 head iceberg lettuce
2 1-pound squabs (2 chicken
   breasts, boned and skinned
   may be substituted)
4 ounces lean pork, diced
1 teaspoon salt
1 egg white
2 tablespoons cornstarch
4 tablespoons oil
1 tablespoon ginger, chopped fine
1 scallion, chopped fine
1 tablespoon sherry

2 tablespoons light soy sauce
1 teaspoon sugar
½ cup chicken stock
4 dried black mushrooms, soaked
   in boiling water 20 minutes,
   stems removed, diced
1 ounce cooked Virginia ham,
   diced
10 water chestnuts, diced
¼ cup bamboo shoots, diced
½ tablespoon cornstarch,
   dissolved in 1 tablespoon water

1. Wash lettuce and separate leaves. Drain and dry. Wrap in cloth and refrigerate.
2. Remove meat from squabs. Dice. Combine with pork. Mix with salt, egg white, and cornstarch.
3. Put 2 tablespoons oil in heated wok. Stir-fry ginger and scallion 30 seconds. Add squab and pork mixture. Stir-fry on high heat 1 minute. Add sherry, soy sauce, sugar, and stock. Cook 1 minute. Set aside.
4. Heat 2 tablespoons oil in wok. Stir-fry mushrooms, ham, water chestnuts, and bamboo shoots. Add squab mixture. Stir-fry on high heat 1 minute. Thicken liquid with dissolved cornstarch.
5. Place entire mixture in center of platter. Arrange lettuce leaves around it. Hot mixture is rolled in lettuce and eaten with fingers.

May be prepared in advance through step 3, or frozen after step 4.

Serves 4 to 6

6

Beef

For many centuries the Buddhists would not eat beef—they considered cows useful only for plowing the fields. Even today, when you say "meat" the Chinese tend to think "pork." But over the years there has been a growing acceptance of beef.

The beef cuts commonly used in Chinese recipes are:

  flank steak, which is easily sliced;

  top sirloin, which has little waste and is tender; and,

  tenderloin, which is used for special dishes.

In Chinese cuisine, a mere pound of beef can make four to six servings, especially when it is combined with other foods. The principle of Chinese cooking is to cut the beef into strips, as indicated in these recipes, and to remove all fat and gristle as you cut. You will end up with each morsel tender and succulent. Thus a little will go a long way.

Beef with Bean Sprouts   ALL REGIONS

The Chinese discard both ends of bean sprouts because it gives a more savory appearance. This is a simple family dish but still unique. Chinese cooking is timing; the cooking of both meat and vegetables requires quick movements.

½ pound filet mignon or flank steak, shredded	1 tablespoon sherry
1 teaspoon salt	2 tablespoons light soy sauce
1½ teaspoons cornstarch	1 teaspoon sugar
4 tablespoons oil	1 teaspoon cornstarch,
2 cups bean sprouts	dissolved in 2 teaspoons water
	(if necessary)

1. Combine beef, ½ teaspoon of salt, cornstarch, and 1 tablespoon of oil. Mix well with hand.
2. Heat 2 tablespoons of oil in wok. When hot, stir-fry beef 1 minute. Remove, set aside, and wipe out wok.
3. Heat 1 tablespoon oil in wok. Stir-fry bean sprouts over high flame. Add ½ teaspoon salt. Stir-fry 30 seconds. Add beef, sherry, soy sauce, and sugar. Stir constantly 5 seconds. If mixture is too watery, thicken with dissolved cornstarch.

Shredding may be done in advance. Do not freeze.

Serves 4 to 6

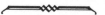

Do not keep eating until your stomach is full. Reserve 30 percent.

Beef with Cauliflower and Peas   SHANGHAI

This is a colorful dish that is simple to prepare and delicious.

½ pound flank steak, cut in
    strips ⅛-inch thick,
    1½ inches long, and ¾-inch
    wide
1 teaspoon salt
1½ teaspoons cornstarch
4 tablespoons oil
½ head cauliflower
½ carrot, sliced thin
Water
¼ cup frozen peas
1 tablespoon sherry

Sauce:

2 tablespoons light soy sauce
¼ cup chicken stock
½ teaspoon sugar
1 teaspoon cornstarch

1. Combine beef with ½ teaspoon of salt, cornstarch, and 1 tablespoon of oil. Mix well with hand.
2. Separate cauliflower into flowerets. Cook cauliflower and carrot in boiling water 10 minutes. Drain.
3. Plunge peas into boiling water 1 second. Rinse with cold water. Drain.
4. Heat wok. Add 2 tablespoons of oil. Fry beef on high flame 1 minute. Add sherry. Cook 1 second. Remove. Set aside.
5. Combine sauce ingredients in a bowl.
6. Reheat wok. Add 1 tablespoon oil. Stir-fry carrots, cauliflower, and peas for 5 seconds. Add ½ teaspoon salt. Add beef. Quickly pour in sauce mixture. Stir-fry 1 minute on high flame.

May be prepared in advance through step 3, or frozen after step 6.

Serves 4 to 6

Beef Chop Suey

I do not consider this an authentic Chinese recipe. However, the demands of my students who love this dish made me include it.

1 pound flank steak
1 teaspoon salt
1 egg white
1 tablespoon cornstarch
2 to 4 cups oil for deep-frying
1 bunch bok choy (Chinese green),
    cut into 1-inch pieces
½ cup celery, cubed
½ cup onions, cubed

½ cup fresh sliced mushrooms
2 cups bean sprouts
2 tablespoons light soy sauce
1 tablespoon sherry
½ teaspoon sugar
4 tablespoons chicken stock
1 tablespoon cornstarch,
    dissolved in 1 tablespoon water

1. Slice beef thin (⅛-inch thick, 1½-inches long, ¾-inch wide).
2. Combine beef, salt, egg white, and cornstarch. Mix well with hand.
3. Fry beef in deep oil 1 minute. Drain.
4. Reheat 2 tablespoons of oil in wok. Stir-fry bok choy, celery, and onions 2 minutes. Remove.
5. Reheat 2 more tablespoons oil in wok. Stir-fry mushrooms and bean sprouts 1 minute. Add bok choy, celery, and onions. Stir-fry 30 seconds.
6. Add beef, soy sauce, sherry, and sugar. Add stock. Stir-fry 2 minutes. Add dissolved cornstarch. Cook 1 minute.

All cutting may be done in advance. Do not freeze.

Serves 4 to 6

Beef with Crullers   CANTON

At first glance this recipe may seem difficult; it calls for Chinese crullers. These are really rectangular doughnuts about 6" to 9" long. Do not be discouraged if you cannot find them: you can substitute unsweetened doughnuts or won ton wrappers. The success of this dish depends upon technique and skill. But it is a well-flavored, hearty beef entrée with a rich brown sauce that everyone loves.

1 pound flank steak, julienne	1 slice ginger, chopped fine
1 teaspoon ginger juice (use garlic press)	1 tablespoon scallion, chopped fine
½ teaspoon salt	1 tablespoon light soy sauce
1 tablespoon cornstarch	1 tablespoon chicken stock
1 egg white	2 tablespoons oyster sauce
1 Chinese cruller or 10 won ton wrappers	1 clove garlic, chopped fine
	1 tablespoon sherry
2 to 4 cups oil for deep-frying	pinch of sugar

1. Combine beef with ginger juice, salt, cornstarch, and egg white. Mix well with hand.
2. Slice cruller or won ton wrappers into pieces 1 inch long. Deep-fry crullers or won ton wrappers 30 seconds, until golden brown. Drain. Keep warm in 200-degree oven.
3. Deep-fry beef in same hot oil until color changes, about 1 minute. Drain. Set beef aside.
4. Reheat 2 tablespoons of oil in clean wok. Add ginger and scallions. Stir-fry 30 seconds. Add last 6 ingredients. Bring to boil. Stir-fry quickly until thoroughly heated. Add beef. Stir-fry 30 seconds.
5. Add cruller or won ton wrappers. Stir-fry 1 second. Remove to platter.

May be prepared in advance through step 1 and cruller or won ton wrappers may be sliced. Do not freeze.

Serves 4 to 6

Beef with Onions   SHANGHAI

This is a very quick dish—good for unexpected guests—that transforms ordinary ingredients into something surprising. Serve on a bed of rice.

1 pound beef (flank or top sirloin steak), julienne	2 to 4 cups oil for deep-frying
½ teaspoon salt	3 or 4 onions, sliced
1 egg white	1 tablespoon wine or dry sherry
1 tablespoon cornstarch	1 tablespoon sugar
	4 tablespoons dark soy sauce

1. Combine beef, salt, egg white, and cornstarch. Mix well with hand.
2. Heat oil in wok. Deep-fry beef until it is seared. Drain.
3. Reheat 2 tablespoons of oil in wok. Add onions. Stir-fry until soft and well-browned, about 20 minutes.
4. Add beef. Add sherry, sugar, and soy sauce. Stir-fry 1 minute, until beef is glazed and brown.

May be prepared in advance through step 3, or frozen after step 4.

Serves 4 to 6

Beef with Oyster Sauce   CANTON

An easy, tasty dish to prepare that's good for beginners.

1 pound flank steak, cut ⅛-inch thick, 1½ inches long, ¾-inch wide	4 tablespoons chicken stock
	3 strips ginger, julienne
	3 scallions, julienne
1 teaspoon salt	1 clove garlic, minced
1 egg white	3 tablespoons oyster sauce
1 tablespoon cornstarch	1 tablespoon light soy sauce
2 to 4 cups oil for deep-frying	1 tablespoon sugar
½ pound asparagus, cut diagonally	1 tablespoon sherry

1. Combine beef, salt, egg white, and cornstarch. Mix well with hand. Set aside 30 minutes.
2. Heat oil to 350 degrees in wok. Deep-fry beef until color changes. Drain and set aside.

3. Reheat 2 tablespoons oil in wok. Stir-fry asparagus 30 seconds.
4. Add 2 tablespoons of stock.   Cook about 1 minute, until crunchy. Remove and set aside.
5. Reheat 1 tablespoon oil in wok. Stir-fry ginger, scallions, and garlic 30 seconds.
6. Add oyster sauce, soy sauce, sugar, sherry, and 2 tablespoons stock.
7. Add asparagus. When sauce boils, add beef. Stir-fry quickly. Serve immediately.

May be prepared in advance through step 6. Do not freeze.

Serves 4 to 6

Beef with Snow Peas (Pea Pods)   CANTON

This is a two-minute dish that shows the great skills of the Chinese for varying beef.

½ pound snow peas (pea pods)
1 pound flank steak
1 egg white
1 tablespoon dark soy sauce
1 tablespoon cornstarch

1 cup oil
¾ teaspoon salt
½ teaspoon sugar
1 tablespoon sherry
½ teaspoon cornstarch, dissolved
    in 2 tablespoons water

1. Trim and string snow peas.
2. Cut beef ⅛-inch thick, 1½-inches long, and ¾-inch wide. Combine beef with egg white, soy sauce, and cornstarch. Mix well with hand.
3. Heat 1 cup oil in wok. When it is hot, pour in coated beef. Stir-fry 30 seconds. Drain and remove beef.
4. Reheat 2 tablespoons of oil in wok. When hot, add snow peas. Stir-fry about 20 seconds.
5. Add salt, sugar, and sherry. Add beef. Stir-fry over high heat about 1 minute. Add dissolved cornstarch. Toss quickly until thickened.

May be prepared in advance through step 3. Do not freeze.

Serves 4 to 6

Beef with String Beans   SHANGHAI

Some dishes do not require a great deal of effort yet result in perfection. This is one of them. The secret is the timing. The wok must be heated first so that the intense heat seals in the juice and flavor. This also retains the nutrition value.

1 pound flank steak	1 tablespoon sherry
1 teaspoon salt	2 tablespoons light soy sauce
½ tablespoon cornstarch	1 teaspoon sugar
4 tablespoons oil	4 tablespoons chicken stock
½ pound string beans	1 teaspoon cornstarch,
1 cup water	dissolved in 1 teaspoon water
¼ teaspoon soda	

1. Cut beef ⅛-inch thick, 1½-inches long, and ¾-inch wide. Combine with ½ teaspoon salt, cornstarch, and 1 tablespoon of oil. Mix well with hand. Set aside.
2. Trim and string beans. Cut them 1½ inches long.
3. Cook string beans in 1 cup boiling water with soda 2 minutes. Rinse in cold water. Drain.
4. Heat wok. Add 2 tablespoons of oil and heat to smoking hot. Stir-fry beef 1 minute, until color changes. Remove.
5. Reheat wok. Add 1 tablespoon oil. Stir-fry string beans 6 seconds. Add ½ teaspoon salt. Pour in beef. Add sherry, soy sauce, sugar, and stock. Stir-fry over high flame 1 minute. Thicken with dissolved cornstarch.

May be prepared in advance through step 3. Do not freeze.

Serves 4 to 6

Beef with Szechwan Preserved Vegetable   SZECHWAN

The flavor of Szechwan preserved vegetable is strong and spicy. It goes well with any meat, especially pork, and is another favorite of East and West.

1 pound flank steak
½ teaspoon salt
1 tablespoon cornstarch
4 tablespoons oil

2 ounces Szechwan preserved
    vegetable
1 tablespoon sherry
1 tablespoon light soy sauce
1 teaspoon sugar

1. Slice beef into strips ⅛-inch thick, 1½-inches long, and ½-inch wide.
2. Mix beef with salt, cornstarch, and 1 tablespoon of oil.
3. Wash preserved vegetable in cold water. Drain. Dry on paper towel. Slice julienne.
4. Heat wok. Add 1 tablespoon oil. When hot, add preserved vegetable. Stir-fry 1 minute. Remove.
5. Heat 2 tablespoons oil in wok until smoking hot. Add beef and stir-fry quickly 1 minute. Add preserved vegetable, sherry, soy sauce, and sugar. Stir-fry 1 minute more.

May be prepared in advance through step 4, or frozen after step 5.

Serves 4 to 6

Emotional upset can kill you; hard labor never will.

Beef Szechwan Style, No. I   SZECHWAN

This is a beautiful dish; the vermicelli is white and fluffy and all of the other ingredients are shredded and conform in size.

1 pound flank steak, shredded
1 teaspoon salt
1 egg white
1 tablespoon cornstarch
2 to 4 cups oil for deep-frying

½ cup bamboo shoots, shredded
½ cup green pepper, shredded
1 tablespoon dark soy sauce
1 teaspoon chili paste with garlic
½ teaspoon sugar
½ ounce vermicelli (mung bean)

1. Mix beef with salt, egg white, and cornstarch.
2. Heat oil in wok. Deep-fry beef 1 minute. Drain. Remove.
3. Reheat 2 tablespoons of oil in wok. Stir-fry bamboo shoots and green pepper 30 seconds. Add beef, soy sauce, chili paste with garlic, and sugar. Stir-fry 1 minute. Remove.
4. Reheat 2 cups oil in wok to smoking hot. Deep-fry vermicelli 1 second. Remove to platter. Pour meat over fried vermicelli.

May be prepared in advance through step 2, or frozen after step 3.

Serves 4 to 6

Beef Szechwan Style, No. II   SZECHWAN

Every Chinese knows this exotic dish: it is the most authentic, distinguished Szechwan beef. The meat and vegetables must be cut into the thinnest of slices. This beef is entirely different from that of other schools—it is chewy because it is fried longer than usual but it retains an exotic flavor.

1 pound beef, julienne
1 teaspoon salt
1 tablespoon dark soy sauce
1 egg white
1 tablespoon cornstarch
2 to 4 cups oil for deep-frying

1 cup celery, julienne
½ cup vermicelli (mung bean)
1 tablespoon sherry
1 teaspoon chili paste with
   garlic
½ teaspoon sugar

1. Combine beef, salt, soy sauce, egg white, and cornstarch. Mix well with hand.

2. Heat oil in wok to smoking hot. Deep-fry beef 2 seconds. Drain. Remove beef. Bring oil to boil again and fry another 2 seconds. Drain again. Remove to platter.
3. In same oil, deep-fry celery 1 second. Remove celery.
4. Deep-fry vermicelli 1 second. Turn and fry one second more. Remove to platter.
5. Reheat 2 tablespoons of oil in wok. Pour in beef and celery. Add sherry and chili paste with garlic. Add sugar. Stir-fry 1 second.
6. Pour this mixture over vermicelli.

May be prepared in advance through step 3. Do not freeze.

Serves 4 to 6

Beef with Vermicelli   SHANGHAI

One marvelous thing about Chinese cooking is the quantities used. A small amount of meat and vegetables makes a masterpiece!

½ pound flank steak, shredded
½ teaspoon salt
½ tablespoon cornstarch
2 to 4 cups oil for deep-frying
1 ounce vermicelli (mung bean)
1 tablespoon sherry

1 fresh green pepper, shredded
1 fresh red pepper, shredded
2 tablespoons dark soy sauce
1 teaspoon sugar

1. Combine beef, salt, cornstarch, and 1 tablespoon of oil. Mix well with hand.
2. Heat oil for deep frying. Deep-fry vermicelli 1 second. Turn it over and fry 1 second more. Remove to plate.
3. Reheat 2 tablespoons of oil in wok. Stir-fry beef 5 seconds. Add sherry. Stir-fry 1 second. Remove.
4. Reheat 1 tablespoon of oil in wok. Stir-fry green and red peppers 30 seconds. Pour in beef. Add soy sauce and sugar. Stir-fry 1 minute, stirring constantly.
5. Pour this mixture over vermicelli.

May be prepared in advance through step 3. Do not freeze.

Serves 4 to 6

Beef with Yard Beans   CANTON

Yard beans (long beans) are highly nutritious Chinese beans.

½ pound yard beans
¾ pound flank steak
2 tablespoons dark soy sauce
1 tablespoon cornstarch
2 cups oil for deep-frying

4 tablespoons chicken stock
½ teaspoon salt
1 teaspoon sugar
1 tablespoon sherry

1. Nip ends from beans. Cut them into 1-inch-long pieces. Set aside.
2. Slice beef across the grain very thin. Put into bowl. Add 1 tablespoon of soy sauce, cornstarch, and 1 tablespoon of oil. Mix with hand thoroughly.
3. Heat oil in wok. Deep-fry beef, stirring until it changes color. Drain through strainer.
4. Reheat 2 tablespoons oil in wok. Add yard beans. Stir-fry about 1 minute. Add stock, salt, sugar, 1 tablespoon soy sauce, and sherry. Cook on high heat about 30 seconds. Add beef. Stir-fry about 15 seconds.

May be prepared in advance through step 3, or frozen after step 4.

Serves 4 to 6

If you eat my food, you will be healthy and live a long life.

Braised Beef with Turnips   SHANGHAI

This is a family dish, tasty when served with rice or in a casserole.

1 pound boneless beef shank
2 tablespoons oil
1 thin slice ginger
1 tablespoon sherry

¼ cup dark soy sauce
2 cups water
1 pound turnips, cut into
    2-inch pieces
1 tablespoon sugar

1. Cut beef into 1-inch cubes.
2. Heat oil in wok. Stir-fry ginger 30 seconds. Add beef. Stir-fry 1 minute.
3. Add sherry, soy sauce, and water. Bring to boil. Cover and simmer 1 hour.
4. Add turnips. Simmer 30 minutes more. Add sugar. Bring to high heat for 2 minutes or until gravy thickens.

May be prepared in advance. May be frozen. Reheat before serving.

Serves 4 to 6

Spiced Beef   SHANGHAI

This is a fantastic hors d'oeuvre and is lovely on a buffet table. The Chinese call it "cold plate." It can also be used for sandwiches.

1 slice ginger
1 stalk scallion, cut into fourths
2 tablespoons oil
1½ pounds boneless beef shank
1 tablespoon sherry

6 tablespoons dark soy sauce
2 star anise
4 cups water
2 tablespoons sugar

1. Stir-fry ginger and scallion in heated oil until aroma comes, about 30 seconds. Add beef. Stir-fry 2 minutes.
2. Add sherry, soy sauce, star anise, and water. Bring to boil. Simmer 2 hours. Test with chopstick or fork for tenderness.
3. Add sugar. Simmer a few minutes. Put on high heat until gravy coats beef.
4. Cool beef. Slice thin for serving. Serve cold.

May be prepared in advance through step 4, or frozen after step 3.

Serves 4 to 6

Ginger Beef   SZECHWAN

Ginger is said to be a curative aid for colds, an antidote to food poisoning, and a source of warmth to the body. It also flavors this recipe.

1 pound flank steak
1 teaspoon salt
1 egg white
1 tablespoon cornstarch
2 to 4 cups oil for deep-frying
½ cup preserved red ginger,
    julienne
¼ cup fresh red pepper,
    julienne

1 scallion, julienne
1 tablespoon sesame seed oil

Sauce:

2 tablespoons hoisin sauce
1 tablespoon dark soy sauce
4 tablespoons chicken stock
1 teaspoon cornstarch

1. Trim fat from beef. Cut across grain into strips 3-inches long and 1½-inches wide. Cut again, julienne.
2. Combine beef, salt, egg white, and 1 tablespoon cornstarch. Mix well with hand.
3. Heat oil in wok. Deep-fry beef 1 minute. Drain. Remove.
4. Combine sauce ingredients in a small bowl.
5. Reheat 2 tablespoons of oil in wok. Stir-fry red ginger, red pepper, and scallion 1 minute. Pour in sauce. Bring to boil. Pour in beef. Stir-fry 30 seconds. Add sesame seed oil. Stir-fry quickly until thoroughly heated.

May be prepared in advance through step 4. Do not freeze.

Serves 4 to 6

Chinese Steak   SHANGHAI

The Chinese have never eaten steak as Westerners know it. In preparation, beef always was cut to bite-size in order to be eaten with chopsticks. This recipe was first prepared by my personal chef 50 years ago.

1 pound flank steak
     or filet mignon
2 tablespoons light soy sauce
1 tablespoon sherry
1 slice ginger, pounded
1 stalk scallion, cut into
     quarters
½ teaspoon baking soda, dis-
     solved in 1 tablespoon water
1 egg white
1 tablespoon cornstarch
2 to 4 cups oil for
     deep-frying
2 fresh tomatoes, cut into
     8 wedges

Sauce:

2 tablespoons Worcestershire
     sauce
2 tablespoons tomato catsup
1 tablespoon sugar
1 tablespoon light soy sauce
1 tablespoon red wine vinegar

1. Cut beef into 1-inch cubes. Pound on both sides. Soak beef in soy sauce and sherry. Add ginger, scallion, and dissolved soda. Marinate 2 to 4 hours or until marinade is absorbed. Discard ginger and scallion.
2. Add egg white and cornstarch to beef. Mix well.
3. Heat oil and deep-fry beef 1 minute. Drain. Remove.
4. Pour 2 tablespoons of oil into wok. Add all sauce ingredients. Bring to boil.
5. Add beef and stir-fry on high heat 5 seconds. Add tomatoes. Stir-fry about 2 seconds.

May be prepared in advance through step 4, or frozen after step 5.

Serves 4 to 6

"Mama's" Beef   SZECHWAN

Before I came to the United States, I tasted this in a Szechwan restaurant in China. The name was given by the owner, whose mama had given her the recipe when she was a young girl.

1 pound flank steak	½ cup canned corn
1 egg white	½ cup canned peas
1 teaspoon salt	1 cup chicken stock
1 tablespoon cornstarch	1 tablespoon sherry
2 to 4 cups oil for	1½ tablespoons dark soy sauce
deep-frying	1 teaspoon chili paste with
1 handful rice sticks	garlic
(Py Mai Fun)	½ teaspoon sugar
1 scallion, chopped fine	1 tablespoon cornstarch, dissolved
1 slice ginger, chopped fine	in 1 tablespoon water

1. Cut beef into very small cubes.
2. Combine beef, egg white, salt, and cornstarch. Mix well with hand.
3. Heat oil for deep-frying in wok. Deep-fry beef 30 seconds. Remove.
4. Reheat same oil until smoking hot. Deep-fry rice sticks 1 second. Remove. Set aside.
5. Reheat 2 tablespoons of oil in wok. Stir-fry scallion and ginger 30 seconds. Add corn, peas, stock, sherry, soy sauce, chili paste with garlic, and sugar. Bring to boil.
6. Pour in beef. Thicken with dissolved cornstarch. Stir-fry quickly until sauce is absorbed.
7. Remove to center of platter. Garnish with rice sticks.

May be prepared in advance through step 5 (keep rice sticks warm in oven). May be frozen after step 6.

Serves 4 to 6

Mongolian Beef   PEKING

The green part of the scallion is an important ingredient in this dish. Northerners use scallions in cooking much more frequently than do Southerners.

1 pound flank steak, shredded	*Sauce:*
1 egg white	
½ teaspoon salt	**1 tablespoon sherry**
1 tablespoon cornstarch	**2 tablespoons hoisin sauce**
2 to 4 cups oil for deep-frying	**2 tablespoons dark soy sauce**
½ cup bamboo shoots, shredded	**2 tablespoons chicken stock**
1 cup scallions (green parts only)	**½ teaspoon sugar**
cut into 1-inch pieces	**1 teaspoon cornstarch**
	½ teaspoon chili paste with
	garlic (optional)

1. Combine beef, egg white, salt and 1 tablespoon cornstarch. Mix well with hand.
2. Heat oil for deep-frying. Deep-fry beef 30 seconds. Drain.
3. Reheat 2 tablespoons of oil in wok. Stir-fry bamboo shoots and scallions 1 minute.
4. Combine sauce ingredients in a bowl. Add to vegetables. Bring to boil. Add beef. Stir-fry quickly until thoroughly heated.

NOTE: If you prefer spice, add ½ teaspoon chili paste with garlic.

May be prepared in advance through step 3, or frozen after step 4.

Serves 4 to 6

To understand the culture of a country, you must understand the cooking of that country.

Sate Beef   CANTON

This beef dish is quite popular in Cantonese restaurants. You can buy Sate Paste or Sate Barbecue Sauce in bottles or cans in Chinese markets. Its tasty anise seed flavor is well liked by the Chinese.

1 pound flank steak
1 slice ginger, mashed fine
½ tablespoon dark soy sauce
1 tablespoon cornstarch
½ tablespoon cold water
2 to 4 cups oil for deep-frying

1 red pepper, shredded
1 clove garlic, chopped fine
2 tablespoons Sate Paste
½ teaspoon chili paste with garlic
½ teaspoon sugar
2 tablespoons chicken stock

1. Trim fat from beef. Slice meat across grain and shred very thin.
2. Combine beef with ginger, soy sauce, cornstarch, and water. Mix well with hand. Set aside 10 minutes.
3. Heat oil in wok. Deep-fry beef 30 seconds. Stir constantly. Drain. Remove.
4. Reheat 2 tablespoons of oil in wok. Stir-fry red pepper and garlic 30 seconds. Add Sate Paste, chili paste with garlic, sugar, and stock. Stir-fry 1 minute.
5. Add beef. Stir-fry quickly 1 minute or until thoroughly heated.

May be prepared in advance through step 2, or frozen after step 5.

Serves 4 to 6

Steamed Beef, Szechwan Style　　　　SZECHWAN

This is the most famous dish in Szechwan cooking. It is exotic and very good for a buffet.

½ pound flank
　　steak or filet mignon
½ teaspoon salt
1 tablespoon dark soy sauce
1 tablespoon sherry
1 tablespoon Szechwan pepper oil
　　(See Index)
Pinch of sugar

¼ cup brown rice meal
3 tablespoons oil
2 tablespoons chicken stock
2 small sweet potatoes, sliced
　　½ inch thick
Water
1 bunch bok choy leaves

1. Cut beef into thin slices ⅛-inch thick, 1-inch wide, and 2-inches long. Mix salt, soy sauce, sherry, pepper oil, and sugar. Marinate beef in this mixture 30 minutes. Add brown rice meal, oil, stock. Mix well.
2. Boil sweet potatoes 5 minutes.
3. Fill wok with water to ¾ full. Bring to boil.
4. Put bok choy leaves in bamboo steamer. Place sliced potatoes on top of leaves. Put beef slices on top of potatoes.
5. Place steamer in boiling water in wok. Steam covered 20 minutes. Serve hot from steamer.

NOTE: Although bamboo steamer is preferred, you can substitute by putting ingredients on plate on rack in pot and steam covered over boiling water 20 minutes. Serve directly from plate.

May be prepared in advance through step 2, or frozen after step 5.

Serves 4 to 6

7

Pork and Lamb

When the Chinese say *meat,* they mean *pork,* the most popular meat for them. There are as many ways to cook pork as there are localities. One can almost tell where a man hails from by the pork dish he orders. For instance, Lion's Head suggests a native of Yangchow and Roast Pork, of Canton. A tourist always seems to order Sweet Sour Pork. There are so many different pork dishes that one could almost eat it every day of the year and never tire of it.

However, of all of the pork dishes the simplest, cheapest, and most versatile is shredded pork. Interesting and varied dishes can be created by cooking it with vegetables or other ingredients.

Braised Pork with Brown Sauce   SHANGHAI

Braised pork, so easy to prepare, is very popular in China. Braised pork in any form—whole or in pieces, with such various ingredients as mushrooms, bamboo shoots, or vegetables—is marvelous with steamed rice.

1 pound lean pork shoulder or butt	1 tablespoon sherry
2 tablespoons oil	3 tablespoons dark soy sauce
1 thin slice ginger	2 cups water
1 scallion, cut into 1-inch pieces	1 tablespoon sugar

1. Cut pork into 1½-inch cubes.
2. Heat oil in wok. Stir-fry ginger and scallion until there is an aroma, about 30 seconds. Remove. Leave oil in wok.
3. Reheat wok. Put in pork. Stir-fry until light brown. Add sherry and soy sauce. Stir-fry 2 minutes.
4. Add water to half cover pork. Bring to boil. Cover wok. Simmer pork about 1 hour. (If water evaporates, add a little more.)
5. Add sugar. Bring to boil. Cook until gravy is glazed.

May be prepared in advance. May be frozen. Reheat just before serving.

Serves 4 to 6

It is so healthy to eat with chopsticks. You eat slowly and digest better.

Braised Spareribs with Black Bean Sauce   CANTON

The fermented black beans give a wonderful flavor to these spareribs, which are easy to prepare and delicious, especially with rice.

2 pounds baby back spareribs
2 tablespoons fermented black
   beans
2 cloves garlic, minced fine
2 thin slices ginger, minced fine
2 tablespoons water
3 tablespoons oil
1 cup chicken stock

1 tablespoon sherry
2 tablespoons dark soy sauce
½ teaspoon sugar
1 tablespoon cornstarch, dissolved
   in 2 tablespoons water
2 scallions (green part only)
   cut into 1-inch pieces

1. Cut ribs into 1-inch pieces.
2. Pound fermented black beans with back of knife or cleaver. Add garlic and ginger. Mix well with water. Set aside.
3. Heat 2 tablespoons oil to smoking hot in wok. Add ribs. Stir-fry until they lose red color, about 2 minutes. Remove.
4. Heat 1 tablespoon oil in wok. Stir-fry bean mixture over moderate heat until there is an aroma, about 1 minute. Add ribs. Stir-fry over high heat 1 minute. Add stock. Simmer 35 minutes.
5. Add sherry, soy sauce, and sugar. Thicken with dissolved cornstarch. Add scallions. Cook 30 seconds.

May be prepared in advance. May be frozen. Reheat before serving.

Serves 4 to 6

Eight Precious Pork   ALL REGIONS

This is a traditional dish that every Chinese family knows how to prepare. It can be refrigerated for a week and is delicious with rice, noodles, and steamed buns.

½ pound boneless pork loin
½ pound bamboo shoots
4 dried black mushrooms, soaked
    in boiling water 20
    minutes, stems removed
4 pieces brown pressed bean curd
1 piece Szechwan preserved
    vegetable
1½ teaspoons light soy sauce
1½ teaspoons cornstarch
2 tablespoons dried shrimp
    (soaked 5 minutes in 1
    tablespoon sherry)

5 tablespoons oil
1 tablespoon sherry
2 tablespoons bean sauce
2 tablespoons hoisin sauce
1 tablespoon chili paste with
    garlic
1 tablespoon sugar
½ cup chicken stock
½ cup shelled raw peanuts,
    without skins
¼ cup soybeans, soaked overnight

1. Cut pork, bamboo shoots, mushrooms, bean curd, and preserved vegetable into ¼-inch cubes. Keep separate.
2. Mix pork with soy sauce and cornstarch.
3. Put shrimp in bowl on rack in pot or in steamer. Cover and steam over boiling water 20 minutes.
4. Heat 2 tablespoons of oil until smoking hot in wok. Stir-fry pork until color changes, about 1 minute. Add 1 tablespoon sherry, bamboo shoots, and mushrooms. Cook 1 minute. Remove.
5. Heat 2 more tablespoons oil in wok. Stir-fry bean curd, preserved vegetable, and shrimp about 2 minutes. Remove.
6. Heat 1 tablespoon oil in wok. Add bean sauce, hoisin sauce, chili paste with garlic, and sugar. Stir over low heat 2 minutes. Add pork, bamboo shoot mixture, and bean curd mixture. Add stock, peanuts, and soybeans. Bring to boil. Turn heat to low. Simmer 15 to 20 minutes.

May be prepared in advance. May be frozen. Reheat before serving.

Serves 4 to 6

Four Happiness Pork   SHANGHAI

You will not find this dish on restaurant menus because it is too time-consuming. However, it is as common to Chinese families as roast beef is to Western families. This dish keeps well in the refrigerator for days. It is delicious served with steamed buns and any vegetable dish.

1½ pounds lean pork	**2 slices ginger**
1 cup water	**1 scallion**
2 tablespoons sherry	**2 tablespoons sugar**
6 tablespoons dark soy sauce	

1. Put pork in boiling water. Boil 1 minute. Drain. Rinse in cold water.
2. Cut pork into 2-inch cubes.
3. Put pork and 1 cup water in an earthenware or any other heavy pot. Bring water to boil. Add sherry, soy sauce, ginger, and scallion.
4. Cover pot tightly. Simmer over very low heat 2 hours.
5. Add sugar. Bring to high heat. Baste until gravy coats the meat.

May be prepared in advance. May be frozen. Reheat before serving.

Serves 4 to 6

Concern yourself about others more than yourself.

Fried Three Shreds   PEKING

Here is an extremely healthful dish consisting of three shredded meats and three shredded vegetables. The Chinese frequently eat this as a family meal.

2 ounces chicken breast, shredded
2 ounces lean pork, shredded
1 egg white
½ teaspoon salt
½ tablespoon cornstarch
4 tablespoons oil
1 teaspoon sherry
1 cup bean sprouts
¼ cup bamboo shoots, shredded

4 dried black mushrooms, soaked
   in boiling water 20 minutes,
   cooked 20 minutes,
   stems removed, shredded
2 tablespoons cooked Virginia ham,
   shredded
2 tablespoons light soy sauce
¼ cup chicken stock
1 teaspoon cornstarch, dissolved
   in 2 teaspoons water

1. Combine chicken, pork, egg white, salt, and cornstarch in a bowl. Mix well with hand.
2. Heat 2 tablespoons of oil to smoking hot in wok. Stir-fry chicken and pork 1 minute. Add sherry. Stir-fry 10 seconds. Remove.
3. Heat 2 tablespoons oil in wok. Stir-fry bean sprouts, bamboo shoots, and mushroom shreds. Add pork-chicken mixture, ham, soy sauce, and stock. Continue stir-frying briskly 1 minute. Thicken with dissolved cornstarch. Stir-fry until thoroughly heated.

May be prepared in advance through step 2. Do not freeze.

Serves 4 to 6

Teach the children before it is too late or the blame will fall on the parents.

Lion's Head   YANGCHOW

When the chef who originated this recipe presented it for the first time, the meatballs were so huge that he named the dish Lion's Head.

1 slice ginger
1 scallion, cut into fourths
½ cup water
1 pound ground pork
1 tablespoon sherry
3 tablespoons light soy sauce
1 teaspoon salt
1 tablespoon cornstarch

2 tablespoons cornstarch,
   dissolved in 4 tablespoons
   water
6 tablespoons oil
1 pound bok choy (Chinese green),
   cut into 3-inch lengths
½ cup chicken stock
½ teaspoon sugar

1. Pound ginger and scallion with back of knife or cleaver. Put in bowl with water. Set aside 10 minutes.
2. Strain out scallion and ginger from water.
3. Put pork in bowl. Add scallion and ginger water, sherry, 1 tablespoon of soy sauce, ½ teaspoon of salt, and cornstarch. Mix well with hand in one direction.
4. Form meat mixture into 4 large balls.
5. Using your hands, lightly coat balls with dissolved cornstarch.
6. Heat 4 tablespoons of oil in wok. Fry balls one at a time until they are brown. Baste with hot oil. Remove carefully.
7. Heat 2 tablespoons oil until smoking hot in wok. Stir-fry bok choy 2 minutes. Add ½ teaspoon salt.
8. Put bok choy into heavy pot. Place meatballs on top. Add 2 tablespoons soy sauce and stock. Cover. Simmer 1 hour.
9. Add sugar. Bring to boil 2 minutes. If the gravy is too watery, thicken with a little dissolved cornstarch.

May be prepared in advance. May be frozen. Reheat before serving.

Serves 4 to 6

Mixed Vegetables with Golden Crown   PEKING

When you have finished cooking this mixed vegetable dish, arrange vegetables and pork in three peaks on a platter. Crown each with an egg pancake. This is so glorified that the chef who created it called it "Mixed Vegetables with Golden Crown." Serve with steamed Chinese Pancakes. I personally like this better than Moo Shu Pork. Try it as a change.

2 ounces vermicelli (mung bean)
3 eggs
½ teaspoon salt
1 teaspoon water
3 teaspoons cornstarch
5 tablespoons plus
    1 teaspoon oil
½ pound pork, julienne
1 tablespoon light soy sauce

1 scallion, cut into 1-inch pieces
2 ounces chives, cut into 1-inch
    pieces (optional)
½ pound bean sprouts
1 tablespoon sherry
1 bunch of spinach, stems removed
2 tablespoons dark soy sauce
½ teaspoon sugar
Salt

1. Soak vermicelli in boiling water to cover about 20 minutes. Drain. Cut into quarters.
2. Beat eggs. Add ½ teaspoon of salt, water, 1 teaspoon of cornstarch. Beat well again.
3. Heat a heavy 8-inch frying pan until very hot. Turn to moderate heat. Brush evenly with 1 teaspoon of oil. Pour ⅓ of egg mixture into pan. Whirl around to make a pancake. When it is set, remove. Repeat with remaining mixture, making two more pancakes. Remove to warm oven.
4. Mix pork with light soy sauce and 2 teaspoons cornstarch.
5. Heat 2 tablespoons of oil in wok. Stir-fry scallion, chives, and bean sprouts on high heat 1 minute. Remove.
6. Heat 2 tablespoons oil to smoking hot in wok. Stir-fry pork 1 minute or until color changes. Add sherry and vermicelli. Stir-fry 30 seconds. Remove.
7. Heat 1 tablespoon oil in wok. Stir-fry spinach on high heat. Discard liquid. Add meat and vegetables. Add dark soy sauce and sugar. Stir-fry over high heat 1 minute until thoroughly heated. Season with salt to taste. Stir-fry 5 seconds. Arrange on platter in 3 mounds. Place an egg pancake

on top of each mound.   Delicious served with rice or rolled in steamed Chinese pancakes.

NOTE: Another way of garnishing this dish is to shred the egg pancakes very fine.

May be prepared in advance. Reheat before serving. Do not freeze.

Serves 4 to 6

Peppers Stuffed with Pork   SHANGHAI

Another dish for beginners. Try it on your family—you will be an instant success.

1 pound pork, minced
½ teaspoon salt
3 tablespoons light soy sauce
1 tablespoon sherry
1 slice ginger, chopped fine
1 scallion, chopped fine
¼ cup water

1½ teaspoons cornstarch
8 small green peppers
¼ cup oil
1 cup chicken stock
½ teaspoon sugar
1½ teaspoons cornstarch,
    dissolved in 1 tablespoon water

1. Combine pork with salt, 1 tablespoon of soy sauce, sherry, ginger, scallion, water, and cornstarch. Mix well.
2. Remove stems from peppers. Cut hole at the tops. Remove seeds. Wash thoroughly. Dry.
3. Fill peppers with pork mixture.
4. Heat oil in wok. Stir-fry peppers 1 minute. Add 2 tablespoons soy sauce, stock, and sugar. Bring to boil. Simmer 20 minutes.
5. Thicken gravy with dissolved cornstarch. Stir constantly.
6. Remove peppers to platter and pour sauce over them.

May be prepared in advance through step 4, or frozen after step 5.

Serves 4 to 6

Moo Shu Pork   PEKING

For the past twenty-five years this has been the most popular Chinese dish in the Western world. I consider it irresistible.

4 dried black mushrooms	1 tablespoon sherry
2 tablespoons golden lilies	½ teaspoon sugar
2 tablespoons (after soaking) fungus	½ medium-sized head cabbage, julienne
1½ cups boiling water	¼ cup bamboo shoots, julienne
½ pound lean pork julienne	6 water chestnuts, shredded
4 tablespoons light soy sauce	½ teaspoon salt
½ teaspoon cornstarch	4 eggs slightly beaten
6 tablespoons oil	3 tablespoons hoisin sauce
1 scallion, julienne	Chinese pancakes (See Index)
1 slice ginger, julienne	

1. Place mushrooms, golden lilies, and fungus in separate bowls. Pour boiling water over each. Soak separately at least 20 minutes.
2. Remove stems from mushrooms, hard tips from golden lilies, and hard part of fungus. Discard. Cut ingredients julienne.
3. Mix pork with 1 tablespoon of soy sauce and cornstarch.
4. Heat 2 tablespoons of oil in wok. Add scallion and ginger. Stir-fry 30 seconds. Add pork. Stir-fry about 1 minute or until color changes. Add 1 tablespoon of soy sauce, sherry, and sugar. Remove.
5. Heat 2 tablespoons of oil in wok. Add cabbage, bamboo shoots, water chestnuts, and salt. Stir-fry 2 minutes. Add mushrooms, golden lilies, and fungus. Stir-fry 1 minute more. Remove.
6. Heat 2 tablespoons oil in wok. Pour in beaten eggs. Scramble them very fine. Remove.

7. Return pork, vegetable mixture, and eggs to wok. Heat thoroughly.
Add 2 tablespoons soy sauce and stir-fry quickly.

TO SERVE: Place steamed pancake flat on a plate.   Spread 1 teaspoon
hoisin sauce in center of pancake. Scoop 2 tablespoons of filling on top of
sauce. Roll pancake, folding one end to prevent dripping.

May be prepared in advance. May be frozen. Reheat before serving.

Serves 4 to 6

Pork with Bamboo Shoots   SHANGHAI

*You will be proud of your accomplishment and you will surprise your guests
when you serve this simple dish.*

½ pound pork loin, julienne
1 tablespoon light soy sauce
1 teaspoon cornstarch
4 tablespoons oil
1 thin slice ginger, chopped fine

1 scallion, chopped fine
1 tablespoon sherry
2 tablespoons dark soy sauce
1 cup bamboo shoots, julienne
1 teaspoon sugar

1. Mix pork with light soy sauce and cornstarch.
2. Heat 2 tablespoons of oil in wok. Stir-fry ginger and scallion 30 seconds.
Add pork. Stir-fry until meat changes color. Add sherry and 1 tablespoon
of dark soy sauce. Remove.
3. Heat 2 tablespoons of oil in wok. Stir-fry bamboo shoots 1 minute.
Pour in meat mixture. Add 1 tablespoon dark soy sauce and sugar. Stir-fry
on high heat 2 minutes.

May be prepared in advance. May be frozen. Reheat before serving.

Serves 4 to 6

Pork with Celery Cabbage   SHANGHAI

Pork goes a long way. Here is a well-known Shanghai family dish that is good for topping noodles, rice, or bean curd.

½ pound pork loin, julienne
1 tablespoon light soy sauce
1 teaspoon cornstarch
4 tablespoons oil
1 thin slice ginger, chopped fine
1 scallion, chopped fine

1 tablespoon sherry
2 tablespoons dark soy sauce
1 pound celery cabbage, julienne
2 teaspoons sugar
1½ teaspoons cornstarch, dissolved
    in 1 tablespoon water

1. Mix pork with light soy sauce and cornstarch.
2. Heat 2 tablespoons of oil in wok. Stir-fry ginger and scallion until there is an aroma, about 30 seconds. Add pork. Stir-fry over high heat until meat changes color, about 1 minute. Add sherry and 1 tablespoon dark soy sauce. Remove.
3. Heat 2 tablespoons oil in wok. Stir-fry celery cabbage 2 minutes until barely wilted. Add pork. Add 1 tablespoon dark soy sauce and sugar. Cook 5 minutes.
4. Thicken with dissolved cornstarch.

May be prepared in advance. May be frozen. Reheat before serving.

Serves 4 to 6

Pork with Chives   SHANGHAI

This dish has a lovely, delicate flavor.

½ pound pork loin or butt,
    julienne
½ teaspoon salt
1 teaspoon cornstarch
4 tablespoons oil
1 thin slice ginger, chopped fine

1 scallion, chopped fine
1 tablespoon sherry
2 tablespoons light soy sauce
4 ounces chives, cut into 2-inch
    lengths
1 teaspoon sugar

1. Mix pork with salt and cornstarch.
2. Heat 2 tablespoons of oil in wok. Stir-fry ginger and scallion on

moderate flame until there is an aroma, about 30 seconds. Turn heat to high. Add pork. Stir-fry until meat changes color, about 1 minute. Add sherry and 1 tablespoon of soy sauce. Stir-fry 1 minute. Remove.
3. Heat 2 tablespoons oil in wok. Stir-fry chives 1 minute. Pour in pork mixture. Add 1 tablespoon soy sauce and sugar. Stir-fry over high heat 1 minute.

May be prepared in advance through step 2, or frozen after step 3. Reheat before serving.

Serves 4 to 6

Pork with Szechwan Preserved Vegetable   SZECHWAN

Crispy and tasty Szechwan preserved vegetable makes this a well-flavored dish.

1 cup Szechwan preserved vegetable	4 tablespoons oil
1 pound lean pork, shredded fine	1 tablespoon sherry
1½ teaspoons light soy sauce	1 tablespoon dark soy sauce
1½ teaspoons cornstarch	2 teaspoons sugar

1. Wash preserved vegetable. Pat dry. Cut into fine shreds. Set aside.
2. Mix pork with light soy sauce and cornstarch.
3. Heat 2 tablespoons of oil in wok. Stir-fry pork until it changes color, about 1 minute. Remove.
4. Heat 2 tablespoons oil in wok. Stir-fry preserved vegetable 10 seconds. Add pork, sherry, dark soy sauce, and sugar. Cook 3 minutes, stirring constantly.

May be prepared in advance. May be frozen. Reheat before serving.

Serves 4 to 6

It is important to be dignified.

Pork with Yunnan Cabbage   YUNNAN

Yunnan cabbage is preserved turnips. It is a famous product of this province and it is most flavorful when combined with pork.

½ pound pork loin, julienne
½ teaspoon salt
1 teaspoon cornstarch
4 tablespoons oil
1 thin slice ginger, chopped fine

1 scallion, chopped fine
1 tablespoon sherry
1 tablespoon light soy sauce
4 ounces Yunnan cabbage, julienne
1 tablespoon sugar

1. Mix pork with salt and cornstarch.
2. Heat 2 tablespoons of oil in wok. Stir-fry ginger and scallion until there is an aroma, about 30 seconds. Add pork. Stir-fry until meat changes color, about 1 minute. Add sherry and soy sauce. Stir-fry 1 minute more. Remove.
3. Heat 2 tablespoons of oil in wok. Stir-fry Yunnan cabbage 1 minute. Pour in meat mixture. Add sugar. Stir-fry 1 minute more.

May be prepared in advance. May be frozen. Reheat before serving.

Serves 4 to 6

Roast Pork with Bok Choy   CANTON

This is a colorful, quick, extremely nutritious dish requested many times during my cooking demonstrations in New York.

½ pound roast pork, sliced thin
4 tablespoons oil
½ pound bok choy (Chinese green),
    shredded
¼ pound snow peas (pea pods),
    washed, strings removed
1 teaspoon salt

¼ cup chicken stock
2 tablespoons light soy sauce
1 teaspoon sugar
½ teaspoon cornstarch, dissolved
    in 1 teaspoon water

1. Stir-fry roast pork in 1 tablespoon heated oil about 1 minute. Remove.
2. Heat 3 tablespoons oil in wok. Stir-fry bok choy and snow peas on high heat 1 minute. Add salt.

3. Add pork. Add stock, soy sauce, and sugar. Stir-fry over high flame 30 seconds.
4. Thicken with dissolved cornstarch.

May be prepared in advance through step 1. Do not freeze.

Serves 4 to 6

Shredded Pork with Golden Cap   PEKING

Here is an especially nutritious and well-balanced dish. You can substitute chicken or any meat you like for pork.

½ pound pork, shredded
1 teaspoon salt
1 teaspoon cornstarch
5 tablespoons oil
1 tablespoon sherry
2 tablespoons light soy sauce

½ cup bamboo shoots, shredded
10 water chestnuts, shredded
½ pound bean sprouts
1 teaspoon sugar
2 eggs, beaten slightly with
    ¼ teaspoon salt

1. Mix pork with ½ teaspoon of salt and cornstarch.
2. Heat 2 tablespoons of oil in wok. Stir-fry pork until color changes, about 1 minute. Add sherry and 1 tablespoon of soy sauce. Stir-fry 1 minute more. Remove to plate.
3. Heat 1 tablespoon of oil in wok. Stir-fry bamboo shoots, water chestnuts, and bean sprouts 1 minute. Season with ½ teaspoon salt and 1 tablespoon soy sauce. Add sugar. Stir in pork. Remove to plate.
4. Heat 2 tablespoons oil in skillet. Pour in eggs. Fry without stirring until they form a golden brown pancake.
5. Place pancake on top of meat and vegetable mixture.

May be prepared in advance through step 2. Do not freeze.

Serves 4 to 6

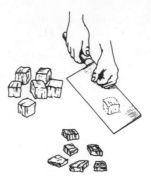

Sweet Sour Pork   CANTON

Here is a well-known dish that is surprisingly simple to prepare.

1 pound pork (loin or fillet), cut into 1-inch cubes	*Sauce*
1 tablespoon dark soy sauce	1 cup water
1 egg white	¼ cup sugar
¾ cup cornstarch	¼ cup vinegar
4 cups oil for deep-frying	¼ cup tomato catsup
½ red pepper, cut into 1-inch cubes	2 tablespoons cornstarch, dissolved in ¼ cup water
½ green pepper, cut into 1-inch cubes	
16 pineapple chunks	

1. Lightly pound each piece of pork with cleaver. Mix with soy sauce, egg white, and cornstarch until evenly coated and well-dredged.
2. Heat oil to 375 degrees in wok. Drop in pork a few pieces at a time. Deep-fry three times, 2 minutes each time, removing meat from wok and bringing oil to boil between each frying. Fry until crispy and golden brown. Drain. Remove.
3. Reheat 2 tablespoons of oil in wok. Stir-fry red and green peppers 30 seconds. Remove.
4. Combine water, sugar, vinegar, and catsup in saucepan. Bring to boil. Stir constantly. Thicken with dissolved cornstarch.
5. Add peppers and pineapple to sauce.
6. Pour deep oil back into wok and reheat to smoking hot. Deep-fry pork 1 minute. Remove to platter. Pour sauce over fried pork.

May be prepared in advance through step 2. Do not freeze.

Serves 4 to 6

Tung Po Pork   YANGCHOW

One day Soo Tung Po, a well-known, revered poet of the Tang dynasty, was served this particular dish in a restaurant. When he asked the name of the delicacy, the chef, thrilled and inspired by the famous poet's presence, at that moment named this dish in his honor.

1½ pounds pork loin	1 tablespoon sugar
Water	1 thin slice ginger
1 teaspoon salt	1 scallion, cut into quarters
2 tablespoons sherry	2 star anise seeds
4 cups dark soy sauce	

1. Cut pork into 6 squares. Rub with salt.
2. Cover pork with boiling water. Boil 1 minute. Remove. Rinse in cold water. Drain.
3. Put pork in earthenware pot or casserole. Add remaining ingredients. Cover. Place pot in steamer. Cover tightly and steam over boiling water 6 hours. Add water when needed.

May be prepared in advance. May be frozen. Reheat before serving.

Serves 4 to 6

Wisdom is a treasure no robber can touch.

Twice-cooked Pork   SZECHWAN

This dish will always win a popularity contest in the West.

1 pound pork loin, butt, or shoulder	1 tablespoon sherry
2 cups water	1 tablespoon dark soy sauce
5 tablespoons oil	1 tablespoon chili paste with garlic
1 leek, cut into 1-inch pieces	2 cloves garlic, minced
½ red pepper, cut into thin strips	1 thin slice ginger, minced
½ green pepper, cut into thin strips	2 scallions, cut into 1-inch
1 tablespoon bean sauce	pieces
1 teaspoon sugar	

1. Cook pork in water 20 minutes. Drain. Cool.
2. Cut pork across grain into paper-thin slices 2 inches in length.
3. Heat 2 tablespoons of oil in wok. Stir-fry leek until wilted, about 5 minutes. Add red and green peppers. Stir-fry 30 seconds. Remove.
4. Heat 2 more tablespoons oil in wok until smoking hot. Add pork. Stir-fry 1 minute. Remove.
5. Heat 1 tablespoon oil in wok. Stir-fry bean sauce on moderate heat. Add sugar. Stir-fry 1 minute. Add pork, leek, and peppers. Cook over high heat 1 minute. Add sherry, soy sauce, and chili paste with garlic. Add garlic and ginger. Stir-fry to heat thoroughly. Add scallion. Stir-fry about 30 seconds.

May be prepared in advance. May be frozen.

Serves 4 to 6

I love all my recipes. I think each one is the best!

Yu Shin Pork SZECHWAN

This is a typical Szechwan dish—sweet, sour, and peppery. Yu Shin means fish-flavored; actually there is no flavor of fish. However, the seasonings can be used as an accompaniment to fish, and the sauce ingredients can be applied to any meat or poultry.

1 pound pork shoulder or tender-
    loin, julienne across the grain
1 egg white
½ teaspoon salt
1 tablespoon light soy sauce
1 tablespoon cornstarch
2 to 4 cups oil for deep-frying
1 cup bamboo shoots, shredded
½ red pepper, julienne

½ green pepper, julienne
2 tablespoons dark soy sauce
1 tablespoon sherry
1 scallion, julienne
½ teaspoon sugar
1 teaspoon pepper oil or chili
    paste with garlic
1 teaspoon red wine vinegar

1. Combine pork with egg white, salt, light soy sauce, and cornstarch. Mix well with hand.
2. Heat oil to 350 degrees and deep-fry pork one half at a time 1 minute or until color changes. Drain and remove meat.
3. Reheat 2 tablespoons of oil in wok. Stir-fry bamboo shoots and peppers 1 minute.
4. Pour in pork. Stir-fry 1 minute. Add dark soy sauce, sherry, scallion and sugar. Stir-fry 30 seconds.
5. Add pepper oil or chili paste with garlic and wine vinegar. Stir-fry 1 minute.

May be prepared in advance through step 2. Do not freeze.

Serves 4 to 6

White Cold-cut Pork with Garlic Sauce   SZECHWAN

If you wish to know the special dish of Szechwan cooking, this is it. Sensational for buffet or as a cold plate for banquets.

3 pounds pork loin with bone
12 cups water
1 cucumber, sliced thin

Sauce:

3 tablespoons garlic,
    finely minced
2 tablespoons sesame seed oil
¾ cup light soy sauce

1. Put pork in roasting pan. Cover with water. Bring to boil. Cover. Simmer 1½ hours on top of stove.
2. Cool to room temperature. Slice very thin. Arrange on platter. Arrange a layer of cucumbers on top.
3. Combine sauce ingredients. Mix well. Pour sauce over pork and cucumbers or serve separately as a dip.

May be prepared in advance, or frozen after step 1.

Serves 4 to 6

Braised Lamb   PEKING

We Chinese believe lamb gives heat to the body. It is, therefore, especially good during the winter months. As it is very tender, many restaurants in China used to camouflage diced lamb as diced chicken, which was more expensive.

3 pounds boned leg of lamb,
    cut into 2-inch pieces
½ turnip, cut into 1-inch
    cubes
Boiling water
2 tablespoons oil
1 stalk scallion

1 slice ginger
1 tablespoon sherry
½ teaspoon salt
6 tablespoons dark soy sauce
1 cup water
1 tablespoon sugar

1. Boil lamb and turnips separately 5 minutes each. Drain. Discard water.

2. Heat oil in wok. Stir-fry scallion and ginger 30 seconds. Add lamb. Stir-fry 1 minute. Add sherry, salt, soy sauce, and water to half cover meat.
3. Cover and simmer 1½ hours. Stir occasionally while cooking to prevent sticking.
4. Add turnip and sugar. Bring to boil. Simmer 20 minutes. Cook until gravy is thickened and glazed (about 5 minutes).

May be prepared in advance. May be frozen. Reheat before serving.

Serves 4 to 6

Mongolian Lamb   PEKING

For those who like lamb, I have included this easy-to-make recipe.

1 pound boned lean lean leg of lamb, shredded

Sauce

1 tablespoon light soy sauce
1 tablespoon cornstarch
4 tablespoons oil
2 cloves garlic, minced
1 bunch scallions, cut into 1-inch lengths
½ teaspoon sugar
1 teaspoon chili paste with garlic (optional)

1 tablespoon dark soy sauce
1 tablespoon sherry
1 tablespoon sesame seed oil
1 teaspoon red wine vinegar

1. Combine lamb, soy sauce, and cornstarch. Mix well with hand. Set aside.
2. Combine sauce ingredients in small bowl.
3. Heat 2 tablespoons of oil in wok until very hot. Stir-fry garlic 30 seconds. Add lamb. Stir-fry until meat changes color, about 1 minute. Remove.
4. Heat 2 tablespoons oil in wok. Stir-fry scallions 30 seconds. Add lamb and sugar. Stir-fry 1 minute. Add chili paste with garlic, if more spice is preferred.
5. Pour in sauce mixture. Stir-fry briskly over high heat 1 minute more.

May be prepared in advance. May be frozen. Reheat before serving.

Serves 4 to 6

8

Fish and Seafood

Fish in the Chinese tradition is a symbolic food: it means good fortune. It also means bon voyage—have a happy trip and a safe return. When children first go to school, they are served a whole fish, symbolic of "a good beginning and a good ending." When honoring someone, Chinese serve the fish with its head pointing toward the special guest.

Curried Shrimp   SHANGHAI

Shanghai is a cosmopolitan city; imported goods were seen in the market there as early as the 19th century. The chefs created quite a number of curry dishes, influenced by India, of which the following is a colorful and well-flavored one.

1 carrot, diced
Water
¼ cup frozen peas
1 pound fresh shrimp, shelled,
     deveined, cut into halves in
     width, then into quarters

1 teaspoon salt
1½ teaspoons cornstarch
2 to 4 cups oil for deep-frying
1 tablespoon curry paste
1 tablespoon sherry
Roasted peanuts (optional)

1. Cook carrot in water until soft, about 20 minutes. Drain.
2. Plunge peas into boiling water 1 minute. Drain.
3. Wash shrimp thoroughly. Wipe dry. Mix shrimps with salt and cornstarch.
4. Deep-fry shrimp 1 minute (until they turn pink). Drain. Remove.
5. Reheat 2 tablespoons of oil in wok. Put in curry paste. Stir 1 minute over low heat. Add carrot and peas.
6. Pour in shrimp. Stir over high flame 1 minute. Add sherry. Stir-fry 10 seconds. Add peanuts, if desired.

May be prepared in advance through step 2. May be prepared in advance through step 6, without peanuts, and frozen.

Serves 4 to 6

Dried Cooked Shrimp CANTON

This is a two-minute dish, a quick and simple way to entertain unexpected guests, yet the flavor of it is beyond your imagination!

1 pound fresh shrimp
Cold water
1½ teaspoons salt
2 cups oil for deep-frying

1 teaspoon black pepper
¼ teaspoon sugar

1. Remove feet of shrimp with a pair of scissors. Make an opening at back and devein. Soak shrimp in cold water to cover with 1 teaspoon of salt 1 hour.
2. Heat oil to smoking hot in wok. Slide in shrimp. Deep-fry until pink. Drain. Remove.
3. Mix pepper, sugar, and ½ teaspoon salt in a small bowl.
4. Reheat 1 tablespoon of oil in wok. Pour in shrimp. Add seasonings. Stir briskly on high heat 1 minute. Serve hot or cold.

May be prepared in advance. May be frozen.

Serves 4 to 6

The good ones will get their rewards in time. The bad ones will get their punishment in time. There is time for everything. If it doesn't come in reality, then the time is not yet due.

Three-Flavored Scallops   ALL REGIONS

The combination of shrimp, scallops, and chicken makes an unusual entrée for a dinner party.

½ pound scallops
2 tablespoons cornstarch
½ pound fresh shrimp, cut into
    halves lengthwise
½ pound boneless and skinless
    chicken breast (1 breast),
    sliced thin
1 teaspoon salt
1 egg white
2 to 4 cups oil for deep-frying
4 dried black mushrooms, soaked
    in boiling water 20 minutes,
    cooked 20 minutes, stems
    removed

¼ cup bamboo shoots, sliced thin
½ cup pea pods (snow peas),
    strings removed
¼ cup water chestnuts, cut
    crosswise into thin round slices
Pepper to taste
Chili paste with garlic (optional)

Sauce:

4 tablespoons chicken stock
1 tablespoon red wine vinegar
2 tablespoons dark soy sauce
1 teaspoon sugar
1 teaspoon cornstarch

1. Rinse scallops in cold water. Dry on paper towel. Put into bowl. Mix with 1 tablespoon of cornstarch.
2. Mix shrimp and chicken with salt, egg white, and 1 tablespoon cornstarch.
3. Mix sauce ingredients in a bowl. Set aside.
4. Heat oil to 300 degrees in wok. Deep-fry scallops, shrimp, and chicken 30 seconds. Drain well. Pour off oil. Wash wok.
5. Reheat 2 tablespoons oil. Stir-fry mushrooms, bamboo shoots, pea pods, and water chestnuts on high heat 1 minute.
6. Pour sauce over this mixture. Stir-fry 10 seconds. Add scallop-shrimp-chicken mixture. Stir until thoroughly heated. Remove to platter. Sprinkle with pepper. Add chili paste with garlic if desired.

May be prepared in advance through step 3. Do not freeze.

Serves 4 to 6

Clam Sycee

Clams stuffed with meat mixture resemble sycee, *the silver or gold bullion used as money in old China. It was customary during the Chinese New Year, therefore, to serve this dish as a symbol of wealth and prosperity.*

2 pounds clams	1 tablespoon cornstarch
4 cups water	3 tablespoons light soy sauce
2 tablespoons sherry	2 tablespoons cornstarch, dissolved
1 scallion, cut in half	in 2 tablespoons water
1 slice ginger	2 tablespoons oil
1 pound ground pork	1 cup chicken stock
1 teaspoon salt	1 teaspoon sugar

1. Soak clams in shells in water 20 minutes. Wash and drain.
2. Put clams into bowl. Add 1 tablespoon of sherry, scallion, and ginger.
3. Place bowl on steamer rack over boiling water. Steam 10 minutes or until clams open. Remove from shells. Chop fine. Leave shells whole.
4. Combine pork with 1 tablespoon sherry, salt, cornstarch, and 1 tablespoon of soy sauce. Add chopped clams and mix.
5. Stuff clam shells with this mixture. Smooth tops with dissolved cornstarch.
6. Heat oil in wok. Fry clams meat side down until light brown. Add stock, 2 tablespoons soy sauce, and sugar. Cover. Cook 20 minutes. Thicken liquid with remaining dissolved cornstarch.

May be prepared in advance through step 5 and refrigerated, or frozen after step 6.

Serves 4 to 6

Do not withdraw your hand when people need help.

Crab Meat with Celery Cabbage   SHANGHAI

Crab is a great delicacy in both the East and West. It is the sweetest-tasting seafood; nothing surpasses its flavor.

1 pound head of celery cabbage
4 tablespoons oil
½ teaspoon salt
1 cup chicken stock
1 slice ginger, chopped fine
1 scallion, chopped fine
1 cup fresh crab meat, cooked

1 tablespoon sherry
1 tablespoon light soy sauce
¼ teaspoon sugar
1 tablespoon cornstarch,
    dissolved in 1 tablespoon water
Pepper to taste

1. Wash and cut cabbage into quarters. Discard heart. Cut quarters into pieces 2 inches long.
2. Heat 2 tablespoons of oil in wok. Stir-fry cabbage until soft. Add salt and ½ cup of stock. Cook 3 minutes. Remove.
3. Heat 2 tablespoons oil in wok. Add ginger and scallion. Stir-fry until there is an aroma, about 30 seconds. Pour in crab meat. Stir-fry 30 seconds. Add sherry, soy sauce, and sugar. Remove.
4. Return cabbage to wok. Pour crab meat mixture over cabbage. Add ½ cup stock. Bring to boil. Thicken with dissolved cornstarch. Sprinkle with pepper to taste.

May be prepared in advance through step 3 and refrigerated, or frozen after step 4.

Serves 4 to 6

Fillet of Sole Stuffed with Ham and Mushrooms YANGCHOW

Though one might think this dish was gourmet French, it was made in China during the Ching dynasty more than 150 years ago. To avoid breaking them, the fish rolls must be fried with care. Prepare this and you will be established as a sophisticated host or hostess.

1 pound fish fillet
   (sole or flounder)
1 teaspoon salt
1 tablespoon sherry
1 ounce Virginia ham
4 black dried mushrooms, soaked
   in boiling water 20 mimutes,
   stems removed
Water
1 egg white

1 tablespoon cornstarch
¼ cup bamboo shoots,
   shredded
2 to 4 cups oil for
   deep-frying
1 green pepper, shredded
1 red pepper, shredded
1 cup chicken stock
1 tablespoon cornstarch,
     dissolved in 1 tablespoon
     water
1 bunch watercress for garnish

1. Cut fish into thin slices about 3 inches long, 2 inches wide, and ¼-inch thick (about 12 slices).
2. Sprinkle ½ teaspoon of salt and the sherry over fish.
3. Cook ham and mushrooms in water 10 minutes. Drain and shred.
4. Beat egg white slightly. Add cornstarch. Brush over fish. Arrange ham, mushrooms, and bamboo shoots on each slice of fish. Roll up fish. Skewer with toothpick. Dip in remaining egg white mixture.
5. Heat oil to 320 degrees. Deep-fry 1 minute, dropping in fish rolls one at a time. Drain. Remove.
6. Reheat 2 tablespoons of oil in wok. Stir-fry green and red pepper shreds 30 seconds. Add stock and ½ teaspoon salt to make sauce.
7. Add fish rolls and any leftover ham, mushrooms, and bamboo shoots. Bring to boil. Thicken with dissolved cornstarch. Cook 2 minutes.
8. Arrange on platter. Garnish with watercress.

May be prepared in advance through step 3 and refrigerated. Do not freeze.

Serves 4 to 6

Fish and Ham Cutlet   SHANGHAI

When cut into miniature pieces, this dish makes a delectable hors d'oeuvre.

6 ounces fish fillet (sole or bass)
1 tablespoon light soy sauce
½ teaspoon pepper
6 ounces cooked Virginia ham
1 egg yolk
1 tablespoon cornstarch, dissolved in 1 tablespoon water
1 egg white, slightly beaten with fork
4 cups oil for deep-frying

Sauce:

1 cup water
¼ cup white vinegar
¼ cup sugar
¼ cup tomato catsup
2 tablespoons preserved mixed vegetables
2 tablespoons cornstarch, dissolved in 2 tablespoons water

1. Cut fish into slices about 2 inches long, ⅛ inch thick, and 1 inch wide. Season with soy sauce and pepper.
2. Slice ham into smaller pieces than fish.
3. Mix egg yolk with dissolved cornstarch.
4. Press ham and fish together with a small amount of this mixture.
5. Dip fish and ham combination into remaining cornstarch mixture, then into egg white.
6. Heat oil in wok to 350 degrees. Deep-fry cutlets until golden brown. Drain through strainer. Remove.
7. Boil sauce ingredients in a saucepan, stirring constantly and thickening with dissolved cornstarch.

To keep fish crisp, serve sauce separately.

Do not prepare in advance. Do not freeze.

Serves 4 to 6

Fish Szechwan Style   SZECHWAN

Lovers of spicy Szechwan food will love this dish.

1 whole fish (1½ to 2 pounds),
    carp or red snapper
2 tablespoons dark soy sauce
5 tablespoons oil
1 scallion, minced
1 tablespoon ginger, minced
2 ounces pork, minced
2 dried black mushrooms, soaked in
    boiling water 20 minutes,
    cooked 20 minutes, stems
    removed, minced

2 tablespoons bamboo shoots,
    minced
1 tablespoon sherry
1 cup chicken stock
1 tablespoon chili paste with
    garlic
1 teaspoon red wine vinegar
1 tablespoon sugar

1. Cut 3 gashes on each side of fish. Rub 1 tablespoon of soy sauce over it.
2. Heat 4 tablespoons of oil in wok. Fry fish 2 minutes on each side. Remove.
3. Heat 1 tablespoon oil in wok. Stir-fry scallion and ginger 30 seconds. Add pork. Stir-fry on high heat until color changes. Add mushrooms, bamboo shoots, sherry, and 1 tablespoon soy sauce. Stir-fry 1 minute.
4. Put fish into wok. Cover with minced ingredients. Add stock and chili paste with garlic. Bring to boil. Cover and simmer 15 minutes.
5. Add vinegar and sugar. Turn to high heat to thicken gravy.

May be prepared in advance through step 3. Do not freeze.

Serves 4 to 6

Ginger is for colds.

Fish With Wine Sauce   SHANTUNG

The Northerners use a great deal of garlic for cooking. When I go to the North, I can always distinguish a man from Shantung by his height, his broad shoulders—and his garlic smell.

1 pound fish fillet (red snapper or sole)	2 cloves garlic, minced
1 teaspoon salt	1 cup chicken stock
1 egg white	¼ cup sherry
1 tablespoon cornstarch	1 tablespoon sugar
2 tablespoons (after soaking) fungus	1 tablespoon cornstarch, dissolved in 2 tablespoons water
Boiling water	
4 cups oil for deep-frying	

1. Cut fish into 2-inch squares. Add salt, egg white, and cornstarch. Mix well with hand.
2. Soak fungus in boiling water 20 minutes. Wash thoroughly. Remove the woody part.
3. Deep-fry fish in wok over moderate heat about 1 minute, or until it begins to change color. Scoop fish into strainer. Drain. Remove.
4. Reheat 2 tablespoons of oil in wok. Stir-fry garlic and fungus 1 minute. Add stock, sherry, and sugar. Bring to boil. Slide fish in.
5. Cook 1 minute, stirring gently. Thicken with dissolved cornstarch.

May be prepared in advance through step 2. Do not freeze.

Serves 4 to 6

Five Willowy Shreds on Sweet Sour Fish   CANTON

Only the Chinese could think of such a poetic name for a fish recipe. Try Chinese Steak with Vegetables as an accompanying dish. Delicious!

1 fish, 1½ to 2½ pounds (red snapper, or sea bass with tail and head)
2 tablespoons sherry
2 teaspoons salt
½ cup flour
4 to 8 cups oil for deep-frying
2 scallions, shredded
2 slices ginger, shredded
¼ cup tomato catsup
½ cup preserved mixed vegetables (if not available, use ½ each of a red and green pepper, shredded)

Sauce:

1½ cups water
6 tablespoons sugar
6 tablespoons red wine vinegar
1 teaspoon chili paste with garlic or 1 teaspoon pepper oil
2 tablespoons plus 1½ teaspoons cornstarch dissolved in same quantity water

1. Clean fish. Cut 3 gashes on each side. Wipe until dry.
2. Rub inside with sherry. Rub outside with salt. Sprinkle flour all over fish.
3. Heat oil in wok. Deep-fry fish 15 minutes, turning every 5 minutes until very crispy. Drain. Remove to platter.
4. Reheat 1 tablespoon of oil in wok. Stir-fry scallions and ginger 30 seconds.
5. Mix sauce ingredients, except dissolved cornstarch, in a bowl.
6. Reheat 1 tablespoon of oil in wok. Pour in tomato catsup. Stir-fry on low heat 1 minute. Pour in sauce ingredients. Bring to boil, stirring constantly. Thicken with dissolved cornstarch. Pour in preserved vegetables, scallions, and ginger. Bring to boil over high heat 1 second. Pour over fried fish.

May be prepared in advance through step 1 and refrigerated. Do not freeze.

Serves 4 to 6

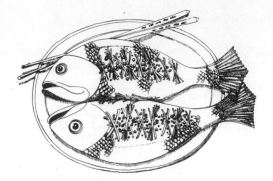

Hangchow Fish   HANGCHOW

There is a Chinese saying, "Above us there is paradise. Below us are Soochow and Hangchow." Hangchow has many scenic spots, one of the most outstanding of which is the West Lake, which teems with fresh fish and shrimp. People go there especially for this outstanding dish.

8 cups water
1 2-pound whole fish (carp or
    lake bass)
2 tablespoons oil
2 tablespoons ginger, shredded
1 scallion, shredded
½ teaspoon pepper

Sauce:

1 cup chicken stock
1 teaspoon salt
6 tablespoons red wine vinegar
6 tablespoons sugar
1 tablespoon dark soy sauce
2 tablespoons cornstarch, dissolved
    in 2 tablespoons water

1. Pour water into a large roasting pan. Bring to boil. Cover and poach fish in boiling water 20 minutes. Turn off heat.
2. Heat oil in wok. Stir-fry ginger and scallion until aroma comes, about 30 seconds. Remove.
3. Combine sauce ingredients, except dissolved cornstarch, in wok and bring to boil. Use cornstarch for thickening. Add ginger and scallion. Bring to boil again.
4. Transfer fish to platter. Pour sauce over. Sprinkle with pepper.

Do not prepare in advance. Do not freeze.

Serves 4 to 6

Imperial Shrimp   SZECHWAN

If you were to vote for one dish as a gourmet's delight, this is it. It has zest. All my students like the shrimp shelled, but the Chinese prefer leaving the shells on: the shell of the shrimp adds to the flavor of this dish. You may shell or not as you please.

1 pound fresh shrimp, shelled and deveined
½ teaspoon salt
1½ teaspoons cornstarch
2 cups oil for deep-frying
¼ cup onions, chopped fine
2 scallions, chopped fine
2 tablespoons ginger, chopped fine

¼ cup tomato catsup
¼ cup chicken stock
1 tablespoon sugar
1 tablespoon sherry
2 tablespoons chili paste with garlic (use 1 tablespoon if you prefer moderate spice)

1. Cut shrimp into halves lengthwise. Add salt and cornstarch. Mix well with hand.
2. Deep-fry shrimp in heated oil 1 minute. Drain. Remove.
3. Reheat 2 tablespoons of oil in wok. Stir-fry onions, scallions, and ginger 1 minute. Add tomato catsup, stock, and sugar. Bring to boil.
4. Pour in shrimp. Add sherry and chili paste with garlic. Stir-fry briskly on high heat 30 seconds.

May be prepared in advance through step 2, or frozen after step 4.

Serves 4 to 6

I will not blame the monk directly. However, I will blame the nun so that the monk hears. He will then feel his guilt.

Lady in the Cabbage   YANGCHOW

Here is a dish that was taught to me by my personal chef in China. When I came to New York, I used it to demonstrate to a class that included many top chefs from American restaurants.

5 small heads bok choy (Chinese greens)	**1 teaspoon cornstarch**
Boiling water	**1 tablespoon (cooked) Virginia ham, minced**
½ pound fresh shrimp, shelled and deveined	**2 tablespoons oil**
1 teaspoon salt	**1 cup chicken stock**
½ egg white	**1 tablespoon cornstarch, dissolved in 2 tablespoons water**

1. Wash bok choy. Remove outer leaves. Use only the hearts. Cut them into 3-inch pieces and split into halves lengthwise. This makes 10 sections.
2. Drop into boiling water. Cook 5 minutes.
3. Plunge bok choy into cold water. This retains the natural green color. Drain. Put on platter.
4. Chop shrimp. Add ½ teaspoon of salt, egg white, and cornstarch. Divide this mixture into 10 portions. Place on ends of bok choy. Sprinkle minced ham on top.
5. Put on plate on rack in pot or steamer and steam covered over boiling water 5 minutes.
6. Pour oil into heated wok. Add stock. Season with ½ teaspoon salt. Thicken with dissolved cornstarch.
7. Remove plate of bok choy and shrimp from steamer. Pour off liquid. Pour sauce over it.

May be prepared in advance through step 4 and refrigerated. Do not freeze.

Serves 4 to 6

In life, there is a bouncing back of things; if you have deep sorrow, then you must have great joy.

Lobster Cantonese   CANTON

This famous dish of Cantonese cooking may be the most popular in the Western world.

2 lobster tails
   (about 1 pound each)
1 teaspoon salt
2 tablespoons flour
1 clove garlic, minced
1 tablespoon salted black beans,
   pounded and soaked in
    1 tablespoon water
2 to 4 cups oil for deep-frying
1 tablespoon ginger, chopped fine

1 scallion, chopped fine
¼ pound ground pork
2 tablespoons sherry
1 tablespoon light soy sauce
1 cup chicken stock
1 tablespoon cornstarch, dissolved
   in 2 tablespoons water
2 scallions, cut into 1-inch pieces
1 egg, beaten

1. Cut each lobster tail in half. Wash thoroughly. Drain. Cut tails into pieces 1½ inches in length, leaving shells on.
2. Sprinkle ½ teaspoon of salt and the flour on lobster.
3. Mix garlic with black bean mixture in a bowl. Stir well.
4. Heat oil for deep-frying to smoking hot. Put in lobster pieces. Deep-fry until shells are red. Drain. Remove.
5. Reheat 1 tablespoon of oil in wok. Stir-fry black bean mixture 30 seconds. Remove.
6. Reheat 2 tablespoons of oil in wok. Stir-fry ginger and scallion until there is an aroma, about 30 seconds. Add pork. Stir-fry on high heat until color changes. Add 1 tablespoon of sherry, soy sauce, black bean mixture, and stock. Bring to boil.
7. Add lobster to meat mixture. Add 1 tablespoon sherry. Cover. Cook 3 minutes.
8. Remove lid. Bring to boil. Thicken gravy with dissolved cornstarch. Season with ½ teaspoon salt. Add scallions. Slowly pour in beaten egg. Stir-fry about 10 seconds. Remove.

May be prepared in advance through step 6 and refrigerated, or frozen after step 8.

Serves 4 to 6

Prawn Rolls   SHANGHAI

A fancy way of making prawns; this dish can also be made with shrimp.

8 prawns (or 16 fresh shrimp)	¼ cup bamboo shoots, julienne
1 teaspoon salt	¼ cup cooked Virginia ham,
½ teaspoon pepper	julienne
¼ cup black dried mushrooms,	2 egg whites
soaked, cooked, stems	4 tablespoons cornstarch
removed, julienne	4 cups oil for deep-frying

1. Wash, shell and devein prawns (or shrimp). Flatten with cleaver.
2. Sprinkle with salt and pepper.
3. Arrange mushrooms, bamboo shoots, and ham on prawns. Roll prawns and skewer with toothpicks.
4. Mix egg whites with cornstarch.
5. Dip prawn rolls into cornstarch mixture.
6. Deep-fry prawns 3 minutes and serve immediately.

May be prepared in advance through step 5 and refrigerated. Do not freeze.

Serves 4 to 6

Shrimp Balls   SHANGHAI

This is a banquet dish that can also be served as an appetizer.

1 pound fresh shrimp,	1½ teaspoons cornstarch
shelled and deveined	1 teaspoon sherry
1 slice of bread (crusts removed),	4 water chestnuts, chopped fine
soaked in water (squeeze out	1 cup cold water
water before using)	2 to 4 cups oil for deep-frying
1 teaspoon salt	Peppercorn salt
½ beaten egg	

1. Wash shrimp. Dry with paper towel.
2. Chop or grind shrimp very fine. Put into bowl. Add bread, salt, egg, cornstarch, sherry, and water chestnuts. Stir vigorously 1 minute until well-mixed.

3. Dip a teaspoon into the cold water. Then dip spoon into shrimp paste and scoop out enough to form a ball the size of a walnut. Repeat dipping process with each ball to prevent sticking.

4. Heat oil to 375 degrees. Drop in balls and deep-fry 2 to.3 minutes. Drain on paper towel.

5. Serve hot with peppercorn salt.

May be prepared in advance through step 4 and refrigerated or frozen. Reheat in oven.

About 30 balls

Shrimp with Peas   SHANGHAI

The preparation of this dish appears easy, but it shows the technique of a fine chef: Timing is the important element. Small shrimp are preferable.

1 pound fresh small shrimp,
    shelled and deveined*
1 teaspoon salt
1½ teaspoons cornstarch
2 to 4 cups oil for deep-frying

¼ cup frozen peas, blanched in
    boiling water 1 minute,
    rinsed in cold water, drained
1 teaspoon sherry

1. Wash shrimp. Change water many times until it is clear. Dry shrimp on paper towel.

2. Combine shrimp, salt, and cornstarch in bowl. Mix well with hand.

3. Heat oil. Pour in shrimp. Deep-fry 10 seconds, or until they separate. Scoop through strainer. Drain and remove.

4. Reheat 2 tablespoons of oil in wok. Pour in peas. Stir-fry 10 seconds. Add shrimp quickly. Add sherry. Stir-fry briskly on high heat 30 seconds. Serve immediately.

---

* If large shrimp are used, cut into 8ths.

May be prepared in advance through step 3 and refrigerated, or frozen after step 4.

Serves 4 to 6

Shrimp in Shell, Shanghai Style   SHANGHAI

Sometimes simplicity is the best. People cannot believe the subtle flavor obtained from this easily prepared dish.

1 pound fresh shrimp in shells	**1 tablespoon sherry**
3 tablespoons oil	**2 tablespoons dark soy sauce**
2 slices ginger	**2 tablespoons sugar**
1 scallion, cut into quarters	**1 teaspoon red wine vinegar**

1. Remove feet of shrimp with a pair of scissors. Make an opening at the back and devein.
2. Heat oil in wok. Stir-fry ginger and scallion until there is an aroma, about 30 seconds. Add shrimp. Stir-fry on high heat 1 minute.
3. Add remaining ingredients. Stir-fry 2 minutes until the sauce is glazed. Serve hot or cold.

May be prepared in advance and refrigerated or frozen.

Serves 4 to 6

Mountains can move, but not your character.

Shrimp with Sizzling Rice   SHANGHAI

This is a dramatic dish. The sizzling rice produces a musical sound.

1½ pounds fresh shrimp,
    shelled and deveined
1½ teaspoons salt
1 teaspoon sherry
1 tablespoon cornstarch
2 to 4 cups oil for deep-frying
6 tablespoons tomato catsup
½ cup chicken stock

1 tablespoon sugar
¼ cup frozen peas, blanched in
    boiling water and drained
1 tablespoon cornstarch, dissolved
    in 2 tablespoons water
1 cup Rice Crispy
    (See Index)

1. Wash shrimp thoroughly. Dry on paper towel.
2. Combine shrimp with salt, sherry, and cornstarch. Mix well with hand.
3. Deep-fry shrimp in oil 1 minute. Remove.
4. Reheat 2 tablespoons of oil in wok. Add catsup. Stir-fry on moderate heat 1 minute. Add stock and sugar. Bring to boil. Add peas and shrimp. Thicken with dissolved cornstarch.
5. Reheat all oil to 400 degrees in wok. Deep-fry Rice Crispy 10 seconds. Drain. Remove to platter.
6. Pour shrimp and sauce over Rice Crispy.

May be prepared in advance through step 3 and refrigerated. Do not freeze.

Serves 4 to 6

Smoked Fish   SOOCHOW

This is a famous Soochow dish. Note the sweet taste, to which the Soochow people seem addicted. (Since the city is also known for pretty girls, one wonders about a correlation between a sweet tooth and beauty.)

Actually, this is not smoked but deep-fried. It is marvelous for hors d' oeuvres. We Chinese serve it for breakfast with congee, as a cold plate for a banquet, or as a topping for noodles.

4 tablespoons dark soy sauce	*Sauce:*
2 slices ginger	
2 scallions	**1 slice ginger, minced**
1 pound fish steaks, sliced	**1 scallion, diced**
½-inch thick (sea bass, cod,	**2 tablespoons sugar**
carp, or black cod)	**1 tablespoon sherry**
4 cups oil for deep-frying	
Anise seed powder (optional)	

1. Combine soy sauce, ginger, and scallions in a flat dish. Marinate fish at least 2 hours in this mixture, overnight if possible.
2. Remove fish from marinade. Set marinade aside.
3. Heat wok until very hot. Pour in oil. Deep-fry fish until slightly dry, about 10 minutes. Drain. Refry if necessary to make it crispy.
4. To make sauce: Reheat 1 tablespoon oil in clean wok. Add ginger, scallion, marinade, sugar, and sherry. Cook until glazed. Dip fish into sauce one by one on both sides.
5. Remove to platter. Sprinkle with anise seed powder if desired.

May be prepared in advance and refrigerated or frozen. Serve hot or cold.

Serves 4 to 6

Smoked Pomfeit CANTON

When I taught this dish to my students, they raved! It is delicious hot or cold. Smoking the fish enhances the flavor. Westerners often serve it with mayonnaise.

1½ pounds pomfeit, flounder,
    or salmon
3 tablespoons dark soy sauce
½ teaspoon salt
1 tablespoon sherry
2 slices ginger, pounded
½ teaspoon sugar
½ onion, shredded

1 scallion, cut into
    4 pieces
2 tablespoons cooked oil
½ cup dark tea leaves
½ cup rice
½ cup brown sugar
6 lemon slices
Mayonnaise

1. Cut fish into 3 pieces. Wash and dry thoroughly.
2. Combine next 7 ingredients and pour over fish. Let stand 2 hours. Turn fish occasionally.
3. Put fish in baking pan. Spread marinade over it. Add cooked oil.
4. Bake fish in preheated, 400-degree oven 20 minutes.
5. Line a large wok with aluminum foil. Put tea leaves, rice, and brown sugar over foil.
6. Arrange 4 chopsticks crosswise on wok, or use a rack. Place fish on chopsticks or rack.
7. Cover wok tightly with a lid that has been covered with aluminum foil.
8. Smoke fish over high heat 10 minutes. Turn to moderate heat for 5 minutes more.
9. Remove to platter. Serve hot or cold with lemon and mayonnaise.

Do not prepare in advance. Do not freeze.

Serves 4 to 6

No man lasts more than a lifetime; his reputation may last forever.

Stuffed Peppers with Shrimp   CANTON

Stuffed peppers are pretty to look at and have both a delightful texture and subtle flavoring. Use this recipe for appetizers or as an entrée.

4 green peppers
1 pound fresh shrimp, shelled
    and deveined
1 teaspoon salt
6 teaspoons cornstarch
1 egg white
1 egg yolk, diluted with 1
    tablespoon water
2 tablespoons black fermented
    beans, pounded

2 tablespoons water
1 clove garlic, minced
1 teaspoon ginger, minced
4 tablespoons oil
½ cup chicken stock
1 tablespoon light soy sauce
½ teaspoon sugar
1 tablespoon cornstarch, dissolved
    in 1 tablespoon water

1. Cut peppers into quarters lengthwise, then cut into 1-inch squares.
2. Grind shrimp in blender or chop fine with knife. Add salt, 1½ teaspoons of cornstarch and egg white. Mix thoroughly.
3. Sprinkle inside of peppers with 4½ teaspoons of cornstarch so that shrimp mixture will stick. Stuff peppers with shrimp mixture. Lightly brush with yolk mixture.
4. Place black beans in a small bowl. Add water, garlic, and ginger. Mix well. Set aside.
5. Heat 2 tablespoons of oil in wok. Put in peppers, shrimp side down. Stir-fry about 1 minute. Carefully turn over peppers. Cook 2 minutes more or until filling is cooked and pepper skins are crispy and tender. Move peppers around occasionally to prevent sticking. Remove.
6. Heat 2 tablespoons oil in wok. Add bean-sauce mixture. Cook over low heat 1 minute. Add stock, soy sauce, and sugar. Slide in stuffed peppers carefully. Bring to boil. Thicken with dissolved cornstarch.
7. Remove peppers, shrimp side up. Pour sauce over them.

May be prepared in advance through step 5, or frozen after step 6.

Serves 4 to 6

Sweet Sour Fish   SHANGHAI

This is one of those simple, never-fail dishes that my students love. Ginger gives an exquisite flavor to the sauce.

1 whole fish, 1½ to 2 pounds, cleaned (sea bass, red snapper, or yellow pike)
1½ teaspoons salt
1 piece ginger, pounded
4 to 6 tablespoons flour
4 cups oil for deep-frying

Sauce:

1 cup water
¼ cup red wine vinegar
¼ cup sugar
1 tablespoon dark soy sauce
4 tablespoons ginger, shredded
2 tablespoons cornstarch, dissolved in 2 tablespoons water
2 scallions, shredded
½ each of a red and green pepper, shredded

1. Rub fish inside and out with salt and ginger.
2. Sprinkle flour all over fish, inside and out.
3. Heat oil to 375 degrees in wok. Deep-fry fish until crispy and brown, 5 minutes on each side. Turn occasionally. Remove with strainer.
4. Bring oil to boil. Deep-fry fish again 1 minute on each side (may need longer frying time to make fish crispy). Drain. Remove.
5. For sauce: Pour water, vinegar, sugar, and soy sauce into saucepan. Bring to boil. Add ginger. Simmer on low heat 2 minutes. Thicken with dissolved cornstarch. Add scallions and peppers. Bring to boil once more.
6. Pour sauce over fish immediately.

May be prepared in advance through step 3 and refrigerated. Do not freeze.

Serves 4 to 6

9

Vegetables and Bean Curd

The Chinese cook their vegetables in oil very quickly. This preserves both the natural bright color and the vitamin content. It also emphasizes the Chinese principle that food must be appealing to the eye as well as to the stomach.

Only the Chinese country people who are too poor to use oil cook their vegetables in water. As a result, the young girls coming to the city fresh from the country have dry, brownish hair and sallow complexions. After a few months of eating city food, their hair becomes black and glossy and their complexions start to glow.

Asparagus with Oyster Sauce   CANTON

This is a quick, gratifying vegetable dish that pleases everyone.

2 tablespoons oil
1 tablespoon ginger, thinly shredded
1 scallion, thinly shredded
1 clove garlic, minced
1 pound asparagus, cut diagonally
    into 1-inch pieces

3 tablespoons oyster sauce
¼ cup chicken stock
1 teaspoon sugar
1 teaspoon cornstarch, dissolved
    in 2 teaspoons water

1. Heat oil in wok. Stir-fry ginger, scallion, and garlic on moderate heat until aroma comes, about 30 seconds. Pour in asparagus. Stir-fry over high heat 1 minute.
2. Pour in last four ingredients. Stir-fry briskly on high heat 2 minutes or until thoroughly heated.

May be prepared in advance through step 1. Do not freeze.

Serves 4 to 6

Bean Sprouts with Green Pepper   SHANGHAI

A wonderful summer dish—when it seems too hot to eat, try this crispy, juicy vegetable dish. It is a cooked salad that is delicious hot or cold.

3 tablespoons oil
1 green pepper, shredded

1 pound bean sprouts
1 teaspoon salt

1. Heat 1 tablespoon of oil in wok until smoking hot. Stir-fry green pepper 1 minute. Remove.
2. Heat 2 tablespoons oil until very hot. Put in bean sprouts. Stir-fry 1 minute. Add salt. Add green pepper. Continue stirring ½ minute. Serve hot or cold.

May be prepared in advance. Do not freeze.

Serves 4 to 6

Celery Cabbage with Chestnuts   SHANGHAI

Until you try this dish, you can't imagine what a delightful combination it is.

½ pound fresh chestnuts or
     dried*
Water
¼ cup oil
1½ pounds celery cabbage, cut
     into 2-inch slices
½ cup water

½ teaspoon salt
2 tablespoons dark soy sauce
1 tablespoon sugar

1. Cut chestnuts in half. Cook in water to cover 30 minutes or until tender.
2. Remove shells and skin.
3. Heat oil to smoking hot in wok. Add cabbage. Stir-fry about 5 minutes.
4. Add water, salt, and soy sauce. Cover. Cook 10 minutes.
5. Add chestnuts. Cover. Simmer 5 minutes. Add sugar. Turn to high heat. Cook, stirring until sauce is glazed.

----

* If dried chestnuts are used, soak in water overnight. Then simmer in water to cover 1 hour.

May be prepared in advance. May be frozen. Reheat before serving.

Serves 4 to 6

Learning is endless.

Braised Turnips with Mushrooms   SHANGHAI

Although some people do not care for turnips, I give you my guarantee that you will enjoy this recipe. The Chinese think turnips are good when you have a cold and that they cleanse your system.

1 pound turnips, cut diagonally   2 tablespoons oil
   in 1-inch pieces   3 tablespoons dark soy sauce
10 dried black mushrooms, soaked   1 tablespoon sugar
   in boiling water 20   ½ cup mushroom stock (liquid
   minutes, stems removed   from cooked mushrooms)

1. Cook turnips in water to cover about 20 minutes or until soft. Drain. Remove.
2. Simmer mushrooms in water to cover 20 minutes. Reserve ½ cup of liquid. (If mushrooms are large, cut into quarters.)
3. Heat oil in wok until smoking hot. Add turnips, mushrooms, soy sauce, sugar, and mushroom stock. Bring to high heat. Cook until sauce is glazed.

May be prepared in advance. May be frozen. Reheat before serving.

Serves 4 to 6

Chinese Greens with Mushrooms   ALL REGIONS

It is important when cooking Chinese greens that the oil be very hot. Stir-fry very quickly and you will retain nearly all the vitamins.

1 pound bok choy (Chinese greens)
6 dried black mushrooms, soaked
    in boiling water 20 minutes,
    stems removed
Water
3 tablespoons oil
1 teaspoon salt

¼ cup chicken stock
½ teaspoon sugar
1 teaspoon cornstarch, dissolved
    in 2 teaspoons water
    (optional)

1. Wash greens. Cut into 1-inch pieces.
2. Cook mushrooms in water to cover 20 minutes. If mushrooms are large, cut into fourths.
3. Heat oil in wok until smoking hot. Add salt and bok choy. Stir-fry 3 minutes.
4. Add mushrooms and stock. Bring to boil. Add sugar. If necessary, thicken with dissolved cornstarch.

May be prepared in advance through step 2. Do not freeze.

Serves 4 to 6

Cold Asparagus Salad   SHANGHAI

Asparagus was used for medicinal purposes during the Ching dynasty—it was thought to be good for the heart. Those who are weight conscious will enjoy this dish without worrying about calories.

4 cups water
1 pound asparagus, cut diagonally
2 tablespoons light soy sauce

2 tablespoons sesame seed oil
¼ teaspoon sugar
1 clove garlic, chopped fine

1. Bring 4 cups water to boil in saucepan. Drop in asparagus. Boil 1 minute. Drain. Rinse with cold water.
2. Mix next four ingredients in bowl. Pour over asparagus.

NOTE: May be kept in covered jar in refrigerator about a week.

May be prepared in advance. Do not freeze.

Serves 4 to 6

Creamed Cucumbers   PEKING

You will probably be surprised to learn that a cream sauce is used in Chinese cooking—this is the Western influence. Here is a banquet dish improvised by the Peking chefs.

1 pound (about 2) cucumbers
Water
2 tablespoons oil
1 cup chicken stock
1 tablespoon cornstarch,
    dissolved in 2 tablespoons
    water

¼ cup evaporated milk
Salt to taste
1 tablespoon (cooked) Virginia
    ham, minced

1. Peel cucumbers. Cut lengthwise into four pieces, and cut these pieces into thirds in widths.
2. Boil cucumbers in water to cover until soft. Rinse in cold water. Drain.
3. Heat oil in wok. Add stock and cucumbers. Boil 1 minute. Thicken with dissolved cornstarch. Bring to boil 1 second. Add evaporated milk. Season with salt to taste. Garnish with minced ham.

May be prepared in advance through step 2. Do not freeze.

Serves 4 to 6

Eggplant with Preserved Szechwan Vegetable   SZECHWAN

A spicy vegetable dish typical of the region. Serve with Lobster Cantonese.

1½ pounds eggplant (banana eggplant if available)	2 tablespoons dark soy sauce
1 cup oil	1 teaspoon sugar
1 ounce preserved Szechwan vegetable, chopped fine	1 teaspoon chili paste with garlic

1. Cut eggplant diagonally into 1½-inch long pieces.
2. Heat oil in wok. Deep-fry eggplant until soft. Drain and remove.
3. Reheat 2 tablespoons of oil in wok. Stir-fry preserved Szechwan vegetable 1 minute. Remove to plate.
4. Put eggplant in wok. Cook over moderate heat 5 minutes. Add last three ingredients.
5. Add Szechwan vegetable to eggplant mixture. Stir. Cook 1 minute. Serve hot or cold.

May be prepared in advance. May be frozen.

Serves 4 to 6

It takes courage to live.

Mushrooms and Bamboo Shoots ("Fried Two Winters") SHANGHAI

The reason this dish is also called "Fried Two Winters" is because the word for winter in Chinese is tung. *Mushrooms are called* tung sun *and bamboo shoots,* tung ku. *Thus, two winters.*

4 tablespoons oil
4 ounces dried black mushrooms, soaked in boiling water 20 minutes, stems removed
1 bamboo shoot, cut diagonally into 1-inch pieces

½ teaspoon salt
2 tablespoons dark soy sauce
½ cup chicken stock
1 teaspoon sugar
1 teaspoon cornstarch, dissolved in 2 teaspoons water

1. Stir-fry bamboo shoot and mushrooms in heated oil 1 minute. Add salt, soy sauce, and stock. Lower to moderate heat and cook 10 minutes.
2. Turn to high heat. Add sugar. Thicken with dissolved cornstarch. Serve hot or cold.

May be prepared in advance. May be frozen.

Serves 4 to 6

Mushrooms with Oyster Sauce   CANTON

These are delicious as a banquet dish or as an hors d'oeuvre with a cocktail.

20 dried black mushrooms
1½ cups boiling water
3 tablespoons oil

2 tablespoons oyster sauce
1½ teaspoons dark soy sauce
1 teaspoon sugar

1. Soak mushrooms in boiling water 20 minutes. Remove stems. Pour mushroom liquid through a fine strainer to remove residue. Simmer mushrooms in this water 1 hour.
2. Heat oil in wok. Add last three ingredients. Pour in mushrooms and liquid.
3. Bring to boil. Cook until gravy coats the mushrooms. Stir constantly while cooking. Serve hot or cold.

May be prepared in advance. May be frozen.

Serves 4 to 6

Mushrooms with String Beans   SHANGHAI

Here is a tasty dish. The mushrooms give a lovely flavor to the string beans.

20 dried black mushrooms
1 pound string beans
2 cups oil for deep-frying

¼ cup dark soy sauce
1 tablespoon sugar

1. Soak mushrooms in boiling water 20 minutes. Remove stems. Reserve liquid.
2. Pour mushroom liquid through a fine strainer to remove residue.
3. Simmer mushrooms in this water 1 hour or until they are tender. Drain. Reserve liquid. When cool, cut mushrooms into fine shreds.
4. Cut string beans into 1½-inch lengths. Pinch off ends.
5. Heat oil in wok to smoking hot. Add beans. Deep-fry about 5 minutes or until they are wrinkled and soft. Drain in strainer. Set beans aside.
6. Reheat 2 tablespoons of oil in wok. Stir-fry mushrooms. Add soy sauce and mushroom liquid. Cook 2 minutes.
7. Add string beans. Cook 1 minute. Add sugar. Stir-fry 1 minute more. Serve hot or cold.

May be prepared in advance. May be frozen.

Serves 4 to 6

Pea Pods with Fresh Mushrooms   CANTON

Pea pods are also known as snow peas. They are the tender pods of baby peas. Crispy and sweet, they go well with pork, beef, chicken, shrimp or lobster. The color of these pods is green and they are as translucent as jade; therefore, they enhance the beauty of any dish when properly cooked.

¼ pound pea pods (snow peas)   1 teaspoon salt
4 tablespoons oil   2 tablespoons chicken stock
½ pound fresh mushrooms,   ½ teaspoon sugar
    sliced ⅛ inch thick

1. Snip off ends of pods. Wash. Leave in colander.
2. Heat 2 tablespoons of oil until smoking hot. Put in pea pods. Stir-fry 1 minute. Remove.
3. Heat 2 tablespoons oil in wok. Stir-fry mushrooms 30 seconds. Add pea pods, salt, stock, and sugar. Stir-fry 2 minutes.

May be prepared in advance through step 1. Do not freeze.

Serves 4 to 6

Six-Minute Broccoli   SHANGHAI

From ordinary ingredients, the Chinese achieve a handsome platter. Putting toasted sesame seeds on top makes this a party dish.

1½ pounds broccoli   ¾ cup water
3 tablespoons oil   1 teaspoon sugar
1½ teaspoons salt   1 tablespoon sesame seeds,
                                        toasted (See Index)

1. Separate flowerets of broccoli into small pieces.
2. Remove tough skin on stems. Cut stems diagonally into slices about 1½ inches in length.
3. Wash broccoli. Drain.
4. Heat oil in wok. When hot, put in broccoli and stir-fry 1 minute.
5. Add salt, water, and sugar. Cover. Cook 3 minutes.
6. Remove cover. Stir-fry 2 minutes.
7. Sprinkle with toasted sesame seeds.

May be prepared in advance through step 3. Do not freeze.

Serves 4 to 6

Spicy Cucumbers   SZECHWAN

This is a spicy salad to please gourmets.

1 pound small cucumbers for pickling	4 whole dried red chili peppers
1 tablespoon salt	1 teaspoon peppercorns
½ teaspoon sugar	3 tablespoons red wine vinegar
10 slices ginger, finely shredded	2 tablespoons sugar
1 red pepper, finely shredded	1½ teaspoons light soy sauce
½ cup sesame seed oil	

1. Cut cucumbers into quarters lengthwise. Sprinkle with salt and sugar. Stir lightly. Set aside 20 minutes.
2. Rinse cucumbers in cold water. Drain. Squeeze out liquid.
3. Arrange cucumbers in a shallow Pyrex dish. Spread ginger and red pepper on top.
4. Heat sesame seed oil in wok. Stir-fry red chili peppers until dark. Add peppercorns. Pour this mixture over cucumbers.
5. Mix vinegar, sugar, and soy sauce in small bowl. Pour this sauce over cucumbers. Marinate overnight. Serve cold.

May be prepared in advance. Do not freeze.

Serves 4 to 6

Saliva is the extract of one's energy. You talk too much, you become dry—no energy.

Spicy Eggplant   SZECHWAN

Eggplant plays a major role among Chinese vegetables. It contains a great deal of iron, and the Chinese way of cooking it is enjoyed by all people.

1 pound eggplant (Chinese
   preferred)
4 tablespoons oil
2 cloves garlic, minced
1½ tablespoons ginger, minced
2 scallions, chopped fine
4 ounces ground pork

2 tablespoons dark soy sauce
1 teaspoon red wine vinegar
½ teaspoon sugar
2 teaspoons chili paste with garlic
1 teaspoon sesame seed oil
¼ cup chicken stock

1. Slice eggplant diagonally into 1-inch slices.
2. Heat 2 tablespoons of oil in wok until very hot. Stir-fry eggplant about 5 minutes or until soft. Set aside.
3. Heat 2 tablespoons oil in wok. Stir-fry garlic, ginger, and half the scallions on low heat until aroma comes, about 30 seconds. Add pork. Turn to high heat. Stir-fry until meat changes color. Add soy sauce, vinegar, sugar, and chili paste with garlic. Stir-fry 30 seconds.
4. Pour eggplant into meat mixture. Add remaining scallions and stock. Cook and stir about 3 minutes. Stir in sesame seed oil.

May be prepared in advance. May be frozen. Reheat before serving.

Serves 4 to 6

Steamed Eggplant   ALL REGIONS

This delicately flavored dish is a dish for all seasons.

1½ pounds Chinese eggplant	*Sauce:*
1 tablespoon oil	
1 tablespoon garlic, minced	**3 tablespoons light soy sauce**
1 tablespoon ginger, chopped fine	**2 tablespoons red wine vinegar**
	2 tablespoons sugar
	¼ teaspoon salt
	1 tablespoon sesame seed oil
	1 teaspoon chili paste with garlic (optional)

1. Cut eggplant lengthwise into thick shredded pieces. Put on plate. Place plate on rack in pot or in steamer. Steam covered over boiling water 30 minutes.
2. Combine sauce ingredients in bowl. Mix well.
3. Heat oil in wok. Stir-fry garlic and ginger on low flame until aroma comes, about 30 seconds. Pour in sauce. Bring to boil. Remove from heat and cool.
4. Pour sauce over eggplant.

May be prepared in advance. Do not freeze.

Serves 4 to 6

My uncle is 90 years old. His principle of living is laughter.

Spinach With Vermicelli   SHANGHAI

Yet another name for vermicelli or mung bean is cellophane noodles. This dish is rich in iron and protein.

2 ounces vermicelli (mung bean)   2 tablespoons dark soy sauce
4 tablespoons oil   1 pound spinach, washed
½ cup chicken stock   thoroughly, stems removed
                                    ½ teaspoon salt
                                    ½ teaspoon sugar

1. Soak vermicelli in hot water 20 minutes. Drain. Cut with scissors into pieces 3 inches long.
2. Heat 2 tablespoons of oil in wok. Add vermicelli, stock, and soy sauce. Stir-fry gently 5 minutes. Remove to plate.
3. Cut spinach into pieces 2 inches long. Heat 2 tablespoons oil until smoking hot. Add salt to spinach and stir-fry over high heat 30 seconds. Pour in vermicelli. Add sugar. Cook 1 minute, stirring constantly until thoroughly heated.

May be prepared in advance through step 2. Do not freeze.

Serves 4 to 6

Stir-Fried Chinese Cabbage   ALL REGIONS

Green vegetables that are stir-fried in oil retain their green color. Therefore, even pale green cabbage looks more appealing.

1½ pounds Chinese cabbage   ½ cup water
4 tablespoons oil   1 teaspoon sugar
1 teaspoon salt

1. Core and discard the tough part of cabbage. Cut into quarters lengthwise and then cut each quarter in half.
2. Heat oil in wok until smoking hot. Stir-fry cabbage 1 minute.
3. Add salt and water. Cook covered 3 minutes.
4. Remove cover. Bring to high heat. Add sugar. Cook 1 minute. Stir constantly. Serve hot or cold.

May be prepared in advance. Do not freeze.

Serves 4 to 6

Spicy Sweet Sour Cabbage   SZECHWAN

The Chinese serve this as a cold plate. It is a super salad to serve if you like a spicy flavor.

1 pound celery cabbage	3 tablespoons white vinegar
1½ teaspoons salt	¼ cup sugar
2 tablespoons ginger, thinly shredded	1 tablespoon pepper oil (See Index)
1 tablespoon oil	

1. Discard core of cabbage. Cut cabbage into pieces 2 inches long.
2. Put cabbage into a bowl. Sprinkle with salt. Let stand 4 hours.
3. Squeeze liquid from cabbage with hands. Distribute ginger evenly over cabbage. Place in container with cover.
4. Heat 1 tablespoon oil in wok. Add vinegar, sugar, and pepper oil. Turn off heat as soon as sugar is dissolved. Pour sauce over cabbage. Marinate in covered container overnight. Serve cold.

May be prepared in advance. Do not freeze.

Serves 4 to 6

String Beans with   SZECHWAN
Szechwan Preserved Vegetable

Simple as string beans are, we Chinese glorify them in this spicy dish.

1 pound string beans
2 cups oil for deep-frying
1 slice ginger, chopped fine
¼ pound ground pork
¼ cup Szechwan preserved
    vegetable, chopped fine
1 teaspoon salt
1 tablespoon dark soy sauce

1 tablespoon sugar
2 tablespoons chicken stock
2 scallions, chopped fine
2 tablespoons red wine vinegar
1 tablespoon sesame seed oil

1. Wash string beans. Nip off ends and string. Cut into 1½-inch pieces. Dry on paper towel.
2. Heat oil in wok until smoking hot. Slide string beans in gently (be careful—oil splatters). Deep-fry beans until wrinkled, about 5 minutes. Turn frequently. Drain. Remove.
3. Reheat 2 tablespoons of oil in wok. Stir-fry ginger 10 seconds. Add pork. Stir-fry until color changes. Add preserved vegetable. Add beans, salt, soy sauce, sugar, and stock. Stir-fry 2 minutes or until dry. Add last three ingredients. Stir-fry briskly 1 minute or until thoroughly heated. Serve hot or cold.

May be prepared in advance. May be frozen.

Serves 4 to 6

You must be cautious with the one who talks as if he had honey in his mouth.

Ten Fragrant Vegetables   YANGCHOW

Remember that uniform cutting is essential in Chinese cooking. Every vegetable must be cut julienne in this very elegant, delicate, and exotic dish.

3 tablespoons oil
½ cup carrots, julienne
½ cup celery, julienne
½ cup bok choy (Chinese green) stems, julienne
½ cup broccoli stems, julienne
½ cup bean sprouts
2 tablespoons sesame seed oil
4 pieces brown bean curd, julienne
2 tablespoons preserved cucumber, julienne
¼ cup Szechwan preserved vegetable, julienne
2 bamboo shoots (whole green), julienne
4 dried black mushrooms, soaked in boiling water 20 minutes, cooked 20 minutes, stems removed, julienne
1½ teaspoons salt
1 teaspoon sugar

1. Heat 2 tablespoons of oil in wok until smoking hot. Stir-fry carrots, celery, bok choy stems, and broccoli stems 1 minute. Remove.
2. Heat 1 tablespoon of oil in wok. Stir-fry bean sprouts 30 seconds. Remove.
3. Heat sesame seed oil in wok. Stir-fry bean curd, preserved cucumber, preserved vegetable, bamboo shoots, and mushrooms 2 minutes. Pour in first lot of vegetables. Add salt and sugar. Pour in bean sprouts. Stir-fry to heat thoroughly. Serve hot or cold.

May be prepared in advance. Do not freeze.

Serves 4 to 6

Bean Curd

Bean curd is called poor man's meat because it is so economical and high in protein (it contains no fat or carbohydrates). It is, on the other hand, a rich man's delight, due to its smooth texture and its ability to give body to any flavor. It is an old man's favorite, for it melts in the mouth. It is a woman's choice because it is good for the skin. Babies also love it. Thus bean curd may be the most democratic of Chinese foods, giving pleasure to everyone.

Beef with Bean Curd   SZECHWAN

Bean curd may become a staple in your own diet after you have cooked this delicious dish!

4 cakes fresh bean curd	½ teaspoon sugar
¼ pound flank steak	½ cup chicken stock
4½ tablespoons oil	1 clove garlic, finely chopped
1 teaspoon cornstarch	2 stalks scallion, cut into
1 tablespoon plus 1 teaspoon dark	1-inch pieces
soy sauce	1 tablespoon cornstarch, dissolved
2 teaspoons chili paste with garlic	in 2 tablespoons water

1. Cut each cake of bean curd into quarters. Set aside.
2. Cut flank steak across the grain into strips 1½-inches long, ¾-inch wide, and ⅛-inch thick. Combine with ½ tablespoon oil, cornstarch, and 1 teaspoon of soy sauce. Mix well with hand.

3. Heat 2 tablespoons of oil in wok. Add beef mixture. Stir-fry on high heat about 30 seconds. Remove to plate.
4. In clean wok, heat 2 tablespoons oil. Add bean curd pieces. Stir gently. Add 1 tablespoon soy sauce, chili paste with garlic, sugar, stock, garlic, and scallions. Cook 1 minute. Add beef. Pour in dissolved cornstarch. Stir gently until thickened and thoroughly heated.

May be prepared in advance through step 3. Do not freeze.

Serves 4 to 6

Bean Curd Casserole   ALL REGIONS

Bean curd goes well with any meat, seafood, poultry, or vegetable. This is simple to make and everyone loves it.

4 dried black mushrooms
1 box fresh bean curd
4 ounces fresh shrimp, shelled and
    deveined
1 teaspoon sherry
1 teaspoon cornstarch

2 bamboo shoots, sliced into
    ⅛-inch pieces
5 cups chicken stock
½ cup sliced cooked chicken breast
Salt to taste

1. Soak mushrooms in cold water to cover. Let stand overnight. Cook them in same water 20 minutes. Drain. Remove stems. Cut into quarters.
2. Cut bean curd into ½-inch squares.
3. Cut shrimp into halves lengthwise, and each half into four pieces. Mix in bowl with sherry and cornstarch. Set aside.
4. Pour stock into casserole dish. Add mushrooms, bean curd, and bamboo shoots. Bring to boil. Simmer 30 minutes.
5. Add shrimp and chicken. As soon as shrimp turns pink, turn off heat. Season with salt to taste.

May be prepared in advance. May be frozen. Reheat before serving.

Serves 4 to 6

Bean Curd Szechwan Style   SZECHWAN

This bean curd dish is a great favorite of the Chinese.

4 tablespoons oil
1 small slice ginger, chopped fine
½ scallion, chopped fine
4 ounces pork, minced
2 tablespoons dark soy sauce
1 tablespoon sherry
4 pieces fresh bean curd

½ cup chicken stock
1 teaspoon chili paste with garlic
⅛ teaspoon sugar
1½ teaspoons cornstarch, dissolved
   in 1 tablespoon water
1 clove garlic, chopped very fine

1. Heat 2 tablespoons of oil in wok. Stir-fry ginger and scallion 30 seconds. Put in pork. Stir-fry 1 minute. Add 1 tablespoon of soy sauce and sherry. Cook 1 minute. Remove to plate.
2. Heat 2 tablespoons oil in wok. Pour in bean curd. Add 1 tablespoon soy sauce, stock, chili paste with garlic, and sugar.
3. Put pork mixture on top of bean curd. Cook over high heat 2 minutes.
4. Add dissolved cornstarch to thicken. Add garlic. Stir gently into sauce.

May be prepared in advance through step 1, or frozen after step 4. Reheat before serving.

Serves 4 to 6

There are destined times for us to do things—to lose, to find, to laugh, to weep.

Bear Foot Bean Curd   PEKING

This is an interesting name for a simple dish.

4 pieces fresh bean curd
1 tablespoon (after soaking)
   fungus
4 tablespoons oil
4 ounces lean pork, shredded
¼ cup sliced bamboo shoots
2 tablespoons dark soy sauce

¼ teaspoon salt
½ cup chicken stock
1 tablespoon cornstarch,
   dissolved in 1 tablespoon water
1 scallion, cut into 1-inch
   lengths

1. Cut each piece of bean curd into 4 triangles by slicing diagonally into quarters.
2. Soak fungus in boiling water to cover 5 minutes. Drain. Remove the woody part.
3. Heat 2 tablespoons of oil in wok. Stir-fry bean curd until it is light brown. Remove.
4. Heat 2 tablespoons oil in wok. Pour in pork. Stir-fry until color changes. Add fungus.
5. Gently add bean curd to pork mixture. Add bamboo shoots, soy sauce, salt, and stock. Cook 2 minutes until thoroughly heated.
6. Thicken with dissolved cornstarch. Sprinkle scallion on top. Cook 1 minute.

May be prepared in advance through step 4. Do not freeze.

Serves 4 to 6

Buddha's Delight   ALL REGIONS

Even Buddha would have relished this dish. If you wish to be creative, substitute vegetables of your own preference.

2 dried bean curd sheets	4 dried black mushrooms, soaked
2 pinches baking soda	in boiling water 20 minutes,
1 tablespoon hair seaweed	cooked 20 minutes, stems
2 tablespoons tiger lilies	removed, halved
1 tablespoon (after soaking)	4 water chestnuts, cut into
fungus	3 pieces
½ carrot	2 tablespoons dark soy sauce
1 small potato	½ teaspoon salt
12 ginkgo nuts	½ teaspoon sugar
½ pound bok choy (Chinese green)	1 tablespoon cornstarch, dissolved
½ head celery cabbage	in 1 tablespoon water
½ cup pea pods (snow peas)	1 tablespoon sesame seed oil
4 tablespoons oil	

1. Soak dried bean curd sheet with soda in boiling water to cover 15 minutes. Wash gently. Drain.
2. In separate saucepans soak hair seaweed, tiger lilies, and fungus in boiling water to cover 15 minutes. Wash. Drain. Remove woody part of fungus.
3. Cut carrot and potato into pieces about 1½-inches long, ½-inch wide, and ¾-inch thick (about the size of a finger). Cook carrot 5 minutes in boiling water. Add potato and cook 5 minutes more. Drain. Put aside.
4. Shell and blanch ginkgo nuts. (If they are canned, this is not necessary.)
5. Cut bok choy and celery cabbage into 1½-inch lengths, ¾-inch wide.
6. String pea pods. Heat 1 tablespoon of oil in wok. Stir-fry pea pods 1 minute. Remove.
7. Heat 3 tablespoons oil in wok. Pour in bok choy and celery cabbage. Stir-fry 2 minutes. Add dried mushrooms, dried bean curd sheet, carrot, ginkgo nuts, tiger lilies, fungus, and water chestnuts. Add soy sauce, salt, and sugar. Cook 5 minutes.
8. Add pea pods, potato, and seaweed. Cook 2 minutes more. Thicken with dissolved cornstarch. Add sesame seed oil last.

May be prepared in advance. Do not freeze.

Serves 4 to 6

Szechwan Preserved Vegetable with Bean Curd   SHANGHAI

Preserved vegetable is made with mustard greens. It goes well with any meat, vegetable, or seafood and tastes especially good with bean curd.

½ cup lean pork or beef, shredded
1½ teaspoons cornstarch
6 teaspoons dark soy sauce
8 fresh shrimp, shelled and
    deveined
¼ teaspoon salt
5 tablespoons oil
½ cup Szechwan preserved
    vegetable, washed and chopped
    fine

Sugar to taste (optional)
4 pieces fresh bean curd, cut
    into 1-inch cubes
½ cup chicken stock
1½ teaspoons cornstarch,
    dissolved in 1 tablespoon
    water

1. Mix pork with 1 teaspoon of cornstarch and 1½ teaspoons of soy sauce. Set aside.
2. Cut each shrimp into 8 pieces. Mix with salt and ½ teaspoon cornstarch.
3. Heat 1 tablespoon of oil in wok. Pour in pork. Stir-fry until color changes. Remove.
4. Heat 1 tablespoon of oil in wok. Pour in shrimp. Stir-fry 30 seconds. Remove.
5. Heat 1 more tablespoon of oil in wok. Pour in preserved vegetable. Stir-fry 1 minute. (If vegetable is too salty, add a little sugar.) Remove.
6. Heat 2 tablespoons oil in wok. Put in bean curd gently. Add remaining 4½ teaspoons soy sauce and stock. Bring to boil. Add pork, shrimp, and preserved vegetable. Cook about 2 minutes. Heat thoroughly.
7. Thicken with dissolved cornstarch.

May be prepared in advance through step 4. Do not freeze.

Serves 4 to 6

Stuffed Bean Curd   CANTON

This is a nutritious one-dish meal, with vitamins, iron, and protein.

2 tablespoons dried shrimp
4½ teaspoons sherry
2 ounces fish fillet
2 ounces pork
1½ teaspoons salt
Dash of pepper
1½ tablespoons water

4 pieces fresh bean curd
4 tablespoons oil
1 tablespoon light soy sauce
1 cup chicken stock
1 tablespoon cornstarch, dissolved
    in 1 tablespoon water

1. Put shrimp with 1½ teaspoons sherry in a bowl. Place on rack in pot or in steamer. Cover and steam over boiling water 10 minutes.
2. Finely mince shrimp, fish fillet, and pork. Add ½ teaspoon of salt, 1½ teaspoons sherry, pepper, and water. Stir thoroughly. Set aside.
3. Cut each piece of bean curd into 2 triangles. Carefully make an insert on the cut side. Stuff meat mixture into hole.
4. Heat oil in wok. Brown bean curd in oil.
5. Pour soy sauce, 1½ teaspoons sherry, stock, and 1 teaspoon salt onto bean curd. Cook 5 minutes. Thicken with dissolved cornstarch.

May be prepared in advance through step 4, or frozen after step 5.

Serves 4 to 6

Life is sweet. Keep on.

Ipin Bean Curd   PEKING

Economical bean curd is for the masses. But this recipe is an exception: it was first served in the Imperial Palace. Ipin means first rank—and this dish turns a pauper into a prince!

2 pieces chicken fillet (about
   ½ pound)
2 teaspoons cornstarch
2 teaspoons salt
1½ cups cold chicken stock
4 pieces fresh bean curd
3 egg whites

2 tablespoons cooked Virginia
   ham, minced
2 tablespoons oil
1 tablespoon cornstarch,
   dissolved in 1 tablespoon
   water
½ pound pea pods (snow peas)
   or spinach

1. Mince chicken fillet very fine. Add 1 teaspoon of cornstarch, 1 teaspoon of salt, and ½ cup of stock. Stir mixture well or mix in blender.
2. Remove water from bean curd by wrapping curd in a cloth and wringing it. Crumble bean curd.
3. Mix chicken mixture with crumbled bean curd.
4. Beat egg whites stiff. Lightly fold in 1 teaspoon cornstarch and chicken-bean curd mixture.
5. Pour mixture into greased casserole dish. Level out contents. Sprinkle minced ham on top.
6. Place dish on a rack in pot or in steamer. Cover and steam 20 minutes over boiling water.
7. Heat 1 tablespoon of oil in wok. Pour in 1 cup stock. Season with ½ teaspoon of salt and thicken with dissolved cornstarch. Pour over steamed mixture.
8. Heat 1 tablespoon oil in wok. Stir-fry pea pods or spinach. Add ½ teaspoon salt.
9. Garnish the dish with pea pods or spinach in a ring around bean curd mixture.

May be prepared in advance through step 3. Do not freeze.

Serves 6

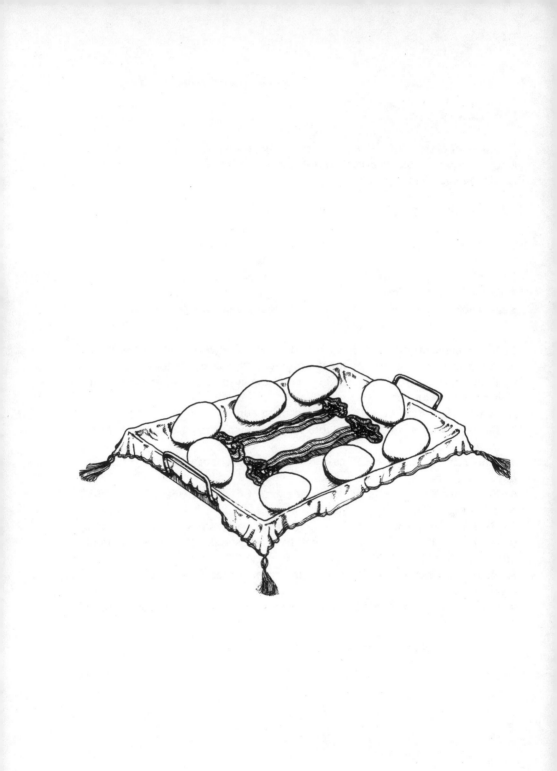

10

Eggs

In China, eggs represent fertility. A charming custom of the Chinese is giving hard-boiled eggs dyed red to show happiness as birth announcements. When an odd number is presented, you know a son has been born. An even number means a daughter.

Another beautiful thing happens when a boy and girl become engaged. The boy's family presents six items of jewelry on a brocade tray surrounded by eggs to the girl's family. These eggs are for good wishes and the wish to have a son as a first-born.

When the couple marry, their bridal bed is red, piled high with twelve embroidered comforters. Dyed eggs are hidden in between them. It is a surprise for the bridegroom and an omen that he will have sons.

Baked Eggs, Peking Style   PEKING

Westerners are well-acquainted with Egg Fu Yung. However, we Chinese have this and many more interesting egg dishes.

4 ounces fresh shrimp, shelled and deveined	1 teaspoon salt
	2 tablespoons oil
5 eggs	1 tablespoon sherry
½ cup chicken stock	

1. Wash shrimp thoroughly. Drain. Dry on paper towel. Chop fine.
2. Beat eggs. Add stock, shrimp, salt, oil, and sherry. Mix thoroughly.
3. Pour mixture into a greased casserole dish.
4. Bake in 400-degree oven 15 minutes. Serve immediately before it falls.

Do not prepare in advance. Do not freeze.

Serves 4 to 6

Crab Meat With Eggs   YANGCHOW

The Chinese love a combination of eggs and seafood.

½ pound fresh crab meat, flaked	1 tablespoon ginger, chopped fine
4 eggs	1 scallion, chopped fine
1 cup chicken stock	1 tablespoon cornstarch, dissolved
2 tablespoons light soy sauce	in 2 tablespoons water
5 tablespoons oil	1 tablespoon red wine vinegar

1. Combine crab meat, eggs, and stock. Add soy sauce. Beat lightly with fork.
2. Heat 1 tablespoon of oil in wok. Stir-fry ginger and scallion 30 seconds. Set aside.
3. Heat 3 tablespoons of oil in wok. Add crab meat and egg mixture. Stir-fry very gently. When mixture starts to set, add ginger and scallion. Cook 2 minutes. Thicken with dissolved cornstarch. Stir in vinegar and 1 tablespoon oil.

Do not prepare in advance. Do not freeze.

Serves 4 to 6

Egg Fu Yung

CANTON

This Egg Fu Yung is different because it is deep-fried and therefore has a very light, delicate texture. Shredded roast pork, beef, chicken, or turkey can be substituted for shrimp.

½ pound fresh shrimp, shelled,
    deveined, cut into small pieces
1 teaspoon salt
1 teaspoon cornstarch
2 teaspoons sherry
5 eggs
1 teaspoon light soy sauce
4 tablespoons oil
½ onion, chopped
1 scallion, chopped
4 water chestnuts, chopped

¼ cup fresh mushrooms, sliced
1 cup bean sprouts
2 to 4 cups oil for deep-frying

Sauce:

1 cup chicken stock
2 tablespoons light soy sauce
1 tablespoon cornstarch,
    dissolved in 1 tablespoon water
Pepper to taste

1. Dry shrimp. Add ½ teaspoon of salt, cornstarch, and 1 teaspoon of sherry. Mix well.
2. Beat eggs in large bowl. Add soy sauce, ½ teaspoon salt, and 1 teaspoon sherry. Set aside.
3. Heat 2 tablespoons of oil in wok. Stir-fry onion, scallion, and water chestnuts 1 minute.
4. Add mushrooms. Stir-fry 30 seconds. Remove.
5. Heat 2 tablespoons oil in wok. Stir-fry shrimp and bean sprouts 1 minute, or until shrimp turn pink. Let cool.
6. Add all ingredients to egg mixture.
7. To make Sauce: Bring stock to boil. Add soy sauce. Thicken with dissolved cornstarch. Season with pepper to taste. Set aside.
8. Heat oil to 400 degrees in wok. Test by adding a piece of scallion (it should turn brown quickly). Gently ladle ¼ of egg mixture into wok. Deep-fry 1 minute until golden brown. Fold over with spatula and fry the other side 1 minute. Remove to platter and keep warm. Continue to deep-fry egg mixture, ¼ at a time. Serve with sauce.

May be prepared in advance through step 6. Do not freeze.

Serves 4

Four Happiness Eggs   SHANGHAI

This is a dish representing the blessings: prosperity, longevity, health, and happiness.

8 eggs	1½ teaspoons cornstarch
6 ounces minced pork	1 tablespoon cornstarch, dissolved
½ teaspoon salt	in 2 tablespoons water
1 tablespoon sherry	3 tablespoons oil
4 tablespoons light soy sauce	1 teaspoon sugar

1. Put eggs in water to cover. Boil 20 minutes. Cool in cold water. Shell and cut into halves lengthwise.
2. Remove yolks. Mash in bowl.
3. Add pork. Mix well. Add salt, sherry, 1 tablespoon of soy sauce, and 1½ teaspoons cornstarch. Stir well.
4. Sprinkle a little dry cornstarch over egg whites. Place meat mixture on them. Smooth tops with dissolved cornstarch.
5. Heat oil in wok. Fry eggs until light brown. Add water to cover eggs, then add 3 tablespoons soy sauce and sugar. Cook over moderate heat until gravy is reduced to half.

May be prepared in advance. May be frozen. Reheat before serving.

16 Egg Halves

At 72 I cannot lose a moment to be unhappy.

Lui Wang Tsai   PEKING

*Many dishes call for egg whites. Here is one that uses yolks only. It is
delicious served over steamed asparagus or broccoli.*

6 egg yolks
¼ cup minced chicken breast
1½ tablespoons cornstarch
1 teaspoon salt
1½ teaspoons sherry

1½ cups cold chicken stock
¼ cup water chestnuts,
   chopped fine
¼ cup oil
2 tablespoons cooked Virginia ham,
   minced

1. Beat yolks. Add chicken breast, cornstarch, salt, sherry, 1 cup of stock,
and water chestnuts. Mix and stir thoroughly.
2. Heat oil in wok. Pour in ½ cup stock. Stir in egg mixture. Stir
constantly while cooking. Cook over low heat until mixture thickens.
3. Remove to plate and sprinkle with minced ham. Serve hot.

Do not prepare in advance. Do not freeze.

Serves 4 to 6

Steamed Custard   SHANGHAI

An ordinary steamed custard is tasty. By adding meat and shrimp, it becomes a delicacy.

5 eggs
1¼ teaspoons salt
1 tablespoon sherry
½ cup chicken stock
2 tablespoons oil
½ teaspoon scallion, chopped fine

½ teaspoon ginger, chopped fine
2 ounces ground pork
1 tablespoon dark soy sauce
4 ounces fresh shrimp, shelled,
    deveined, each cut into
    8 pieces
½ teaspoon cornstarch

1. Beat eggs in bowl. Add 1 teaspoon of salt, sherry, and stock. Beat again.
2. Place bowl on a rack in pot or in steamer. Cover and steam over boiling water 20 minutes. Set custard aside.
3. Heat 1 tablespoon of oil in wok. Add scallion, ginger, and pork. Stir-fry 1 minute. Add soy sauce. Cook 1 minute. Remove.
4. Mix shrimp with ¼ teaspoon salt and cornstarch. Stir-fry shrimp in 1 tablespoon heated oil 1 minute. Add pork mixture. Stir-fry 30 seconds more.
5. Pour meat and shrimp mixture over custard.

Pork may be ground and shrimp cleaned in advance. Do not freeze.

Serves 4 to 6

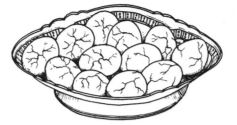

Tea Eggs   SHANGHAI

These eggs are served during the Chinese New Year celebration and symbolize wealth, prosperity, and fertility.

12 eggs   **2 teaspoons salt**
2 star anise   **2 tablespoons dark soy sauce**
¼ cup black tea

1. Cover eggs with cold water. Boil 20 minutes. Cool in cold water. Crack shells but do not remove them.
2. Boil eggs again in water to cover. Add star anise, black tea, salt, and soy sauce.
3. Simmer 2 hours. Keep eggs in juice before serving. The longer eggs remain in the juice, the better their flavor. Serve hot or cold.

May be prepared in advance. May be frozen.

12 Tea Eggs

11

Noodles, Rice, and Congees

Noodles—"mein" in Chinese—symbolize longevity. Therefore, they are traditionally served on birthdays. They may be fried, mixed with meat, or used in soups. They complement any meat or vegetable dish. For perfect noodles, always boil them in a generous amount of water, stirring from bottom. They must never be overcooked. Rinse at once under cold running water or they become mushy. Mix with oil after draining.

Ants Creeping on the Trees   HUNAN

Doesn't this recipe title sound poetic? The ground pork resembles ants and the vermicelli looks like branches of trees. This is an incredibly easy, tasty, and inexpensive dish to prepare.

2 ounces vermicelli (mung bean)
2 tablespoons oil
½ pound pork (or beef), minced

2 tablespoons dark soy sauce
1 teaspoon chili paste with
    garlic
½ cup chicken stock

1. Soak vermicelli in boiling water to cover. Let stand 20 minutes. Drain. Cut into thirds. Set aside.
2. Heat oil in wok. Stir-fry pork to separate grains of the meat, about 1 minute.
3. Add vermicelli. Blend well. Add soy sauce, chili paste with garlic, and stock. Cook on high heat about 2 to 3 minutes. Stir constantly.

May be prepared in advance through step 2, or frozen after step 3.

Serves 4 to 6

Through hardship you learn and get stronger.

Barbecued Pork with Chow Fun   CANTON

Chow Fun is a smooth, slippery rice noodle. It is sold by the pound in a plastic bag. When you cook it with the ingredients below, it will be a special treat. It can be served for breakfast, lunch, tea, or dinner.

**1 pound Chow Fun (rice
    noodles)**
4 tablespoons oil
1 teaspoon salt
1 tablespoon light soy sauce
**2 tablespoons chicken stock
    (if necessary)**

**½ pound barbecued pork,
    shredded**
**½ pound bok choy (Chinese
    green), sliced diagonally into
    pieces about ½-inch long**
½ pound bean sprouts
**1 scallion, cut into 1-inch
    lengths**

1. Cut Chow Fun into pieces about 1½ inches in length and ½-inch wide. Set aside.
2. Heat 2 tablespoons of oil in wok. Add Chow Fun. Stir-fry quickly until it is well-heated. Add ½ teaspoon of salt and soy sauce. If too dry, add stock. Remove.
3. Heat 2 tablespoons oil in wok. Stir-fry pork 1 minute. Add bok choy, bean sprouts, scallion, and ½ teaspoon salt. Stir-fry mixture 1 minute.
4. Add Chow Fun and stir thoroughly.

May be prepared in advance through step 3. Do not freeze.

Serves 4 to 6

Chow Mein with Shrimp and Pork   ALL REGIONS

Westerners eat chow mein frequently, but most of them don't know that it simply means "fried noodle."

½ pound Chinese fresh water
   noodles (medium)
9 tablespoons oil
4 ounces fresh shrimp, shelled,
   deveined, cut into 8 pieces
1¼ teaspoons salt
½ teaspoon cornstarch
½ pound lean pork, shredded
1 tablespoon sherry

2 tablespoons light soy sauce
½ teaspoon sugar
½ pound bok choy (Chinese green)
2 dried black mushrooms, soaked
   in boiling water 20 minutes,
   stems removed, shredded
2 tablespoons chicken stock
1 teaspoon cornstarch, dissolved
   in 2 teaspoons water

1. Drop noodles into boiling water. Boil 5 minutes. Rinse under cold water. Drain. Mix noodles with 1 tablespoon of oil.
2. Mix shrimp with ¼ teaspoon of salt and cornstarch. Heat 1 tablespoon of oil in wok and stir-fry shrimp until they turn pink, about 30 seconds. Remove. Set aside.
3. Heat 2 tablespoons of oil in wok. Stir-fry pork until color changes. Add sherry, 1 tablespoon of soy sauce, and sugar. Stir-fry 1 minute. Remove. Set aside.
4. Heat 2 tablespoons of oil in wok. Stir-fry bok choy 1 minute. Add pork, mushrooms, 1 teaspoon salt, and 1 tablespoon soy sauce. Add stock. Cook 3 minutes over high heat. Thicken with dissolved cornstarch. Pour in shrimp. Bring to boil. Remove. Set aside.
5. Heat 3 tablespoons oil in wok until very hot. Turn down to moderate heat and stir-fry noodles (they will form a cake) until outside is golden brown but inside is soft. Cook 5 minutes on each side. Remove to platter.
6. Place cooked mixture on top of noodles.

May be prepared in advance through step 4. Do not freeze.

Serves 4 to 6

Cold Spicy Noodles   ALL REGIONS

Cold noodles are refreshing for a summer meal, and cold shredded meat and vegetables go well with Chinese noodles.

8 ounces Chinese fresh
    water noodles
¼ cup cold water
1 tablespoon sesame seed oil
1 cup bean sprouts
1 egg
1 tablespoon oil
½ cup (cooked) Virginia ham,
    shredded
1 cup cooked chicken, shredded

1 cucumber, peeled, seeded,
    and shredded
½ cup celery, shredded

Sauce:

¼ cup sesame seed oil
1 tablespoon chili sauce
¼ cup light soy sauce
¼ cup red wine vinegar
½ teaspoon salt (to taste)

1. Drop noodles into boiling water to cover. Cook about 4 minutes. Add ¼ cup cold water and bring to boil 1 minute. Rinse noodles with cold water right away. Drain. Mix with sesame seed oil. Chill.
2. Plunge bean sprouts into boiling water to cover 1 minute. Drain. Set aside.
3. Beat egg. Grease small skillet with 1 tablespoon oil. Pour in beaten egg and fry egg like a pancake. Remove. Shred.
4. Arrange noodles on serving plate. Arrange bean sprouts, ham, chicken, cucumber, celery, and egg on top.
5. Mix sauce ingredients in small bowl. Pour over covered noodles. Serve cold.

May be prepared in advance; pour on sauce just before serving. Do not freeze.

Serves 4 to 6

Egg Noodles in Soup   ALL REGIONS

This delicious soup is a meal in itself. Any leftover chicken or meat can be sprinkled on top.

½ pound egg noodles (fine)
6 cups chicken stock
½ teaspoon salt
2 teaspoons light soy sauce

1 tablespoon sesame seed oil
¼ pound barbecued pork, sliced
⅛-inch thick
1 stalk scallion, cut into 1-inch-long pieces

1. Drop noodles into boiling water to cover. Stir and separate noodles with fork or chopsticks. Boil 4 to 5 minutes. Drain.
2. Transfer noodles to tureen or individual bowls.
3. Bring stock to boil. Add salt, soy sauce, and sesame seed oil.
4. Pour stock mixture over noodles. Sprinkle with pork and scallion.

May be prepared in advance through step 1. Then add 1 tablespoon sesame seed oil to noodles. May be frozen after step 1. When ready to prepare, add 1 tablespoon sesame seed oil and reboil in stock.

Serves 4 to 6

Noodles with Meat Sauce Mixture   SZECHWAN

When Marco Polo first tasted this dish, he licked his fingers—and took "spaghetti" back to Italy!

4 tablespoons oil
¼ teaspoon ginger, minced
1 stalk scallion, chopped fine
½ pound ground pork or beef
1 tablespoon sherry
1 tablespoon light soy sauce
2 tablespoons bean sauce
2 tablespoons hoisin sauce
1 tablespoon sugar
½ to 1 tablespoon chili paste
with garlic

10 water chestnuts, chopped fine
¼ cup Szechwan preserved
vegetable, diced
4 to 6 dried black mushrooms,
(soaked in boiling water
20 minutes, cooked
20 minutes, stems
removed, diced)
½ can whole bamboo shoots, diced
¼ cup chicken stock
1 pound Chinese fresh-water
noodles (medium)
1 tablespoon sesame seed oil
4 to 6 teaspoons light soy sauce
4 to 6 teaspoons sesame seed oil

1. Heat 2 tablespoons of oil in wok. Stir-fry ginger and scallion 30 seconds.
2. Add meat. Stir-fry 3 minutes. Add sherry and soy sauce. Cook 30 seconds. Remove.

3. Heat 2 tablespoons oil in wok. Add bean sauce, hoisin sauce, and sugar. Stir-fry on low heat 2 minutes. Add chili paste with garlic, water chestnuts, preserved vegetable, mushrooms, and bamboo shoots. Stir-fry 2 minutes. Add pork and stock. Cook over low heat 5 minutes.
4. Put noodles into boiling water. Cook uncovered 3 to 5 minutes. Drain. Rinse with cold water, then with hot water. Mix with sesame seed oil.
5. Arrange noodles on platter. Pour meat mixture over them. Serve in individual bowls. Add 1 teaspoon light soy sauce and 1 teaspoon sesame seed oil to each bowl.

Do not prepare in advance. Do not freeze.

Serves 4 to 6

Rice Sticks with Barbecued Pork CANTON

This noodle dish is light, colorful, and easy to digest. It has many ingredients, yet it is simple to prepare.

¼ pound rice sticks (Py Mai Fun)
4 tablespoons oil
2 scallions, cut into 1-inch strips
½ pound barbecued pork, shredded (raw beef or raw chicken can be substituted for pork)
2 tablespoons light soy sauce
5 fresh shrimp, shelled, deveined, cut into eighths

¼ teaspoon salt
¼ teaspoon cornstarch
1 cup bean sprouts
½ cup preserved mixed vegetables, shredded
½ cup red pepper, shredded
½ cup green pepper, shredded
⅛ teaspoon black pepper
½ teaspoon chili paste with garlic

1. Soak rice sticks in boiling water 4 to 5 minutes. Drain. They must dry thoroughly, so it is best to boil them in the morning.
2. Heat 2 tablespoons of oil in wok. Stir-fry scallions 30 seconds. Add pork and 1 tablespoon of soy sauce. Stir-fry 1 minute. Remove.
3. Combine shrimp with salt and cornstarch.
4. Heat 1 tablespoon of oil in wok. Stir-fry shrimp 30 seconds. Remove.
5. Heat 1 tablespoon oil in wok. Add bean sprouts, preserved vegetables, and red and green peppers. Stir-fry 1 minute.
6. Add pork, rice sticks, and shrimp to vegetable mixture. Stir-fry 1 minute. Season with 1 tablespoon soy sauce, pepper, and chili paste with garlic.

May be prepared in advance through step 5 or may be frozen after step 5.

Serves 4 to 6

Rice Sticks with Chicken and Shrimp   CANTON

You must try this sensational dish! Once you use rice sticks in a recipe, you will dream up endless excuses to serve them.

½ pound rice sticks (Py Mai Fun)
1 pound boned chicken
    breasts, julienne
½ teaspoon salt
1 tablespoon cornstarch
1 egg white
2 to 4 cups oil for deep-frying
2 scallions, julienne
1 cup fresh shrimp, cooked, and
    diced

½ cup preserved mixed vegetables,
    shredded
2 tablespoons light soy sauce
¼ teaspoon chili paste with garlic
Salt to taste
Pepper to taste

1. Soak rice sticks in boiling water 4 to 5 minutes. Drain. Let them dry thoroughly. (It is best to boil them in the morning.)
2. Mix chicken with salt, cornstarch, and egg white.
3. Heat 2 to 4 cups oil in wok. Deep-fry chicken until it separates and turns white. Drain. Remove. Set aside.
4. Reheat 2 tablespoons of oil in wok. Stir-fry scallions.
5. Add shrimp and preserved mixed vegetables. Stir-fry 1 minute. Remove.
6. Reheat 2 tablespoons of oil in wok. Stir-fry rice sticks 1 minute.
7. Add 1 tablespoon of soy sauce. Add chicken and shrimp-vegetable mixture.
8. Stir-fry on high heat 1 minute. Season with 1 tablespoon soy sauce, chili paste with garlic, salt, and pepper. (Add more chili paste with garlic if desired.)

Bone chicken and cut vegetables in advance. Do not freeze.

Serves 4 to 6

I choose my friends as I choose my food.

Shanghai Pan-fried Noodles

SHANGHAI

Here is a combination par excellence!

½ pound Chinese fresh-water
    noodles (medium)
½ cup cold water
1 tablespoon sesame seed oil
½ pound pork tenderloin
2 tablespoons light soy sauce
1 tablespoon cornstarch
1 scallion, cut into 1-inch pieces
9 tablespoons oil
1 teaspoon sugar

1 head celery cabbage, shredded
1 tablespoon dark soy sauce
1½ teaspoons cornstarch, dissolved
    in 1 tablespoon water
1 bunch washed spinach leaves
½ teaspoon salt
Red wine vinegar to taste

1. Drop noodles into boiling water. Cook about 4 minutes. Add ½ cup of cold water. Bring to boil 1 minute. Rinse with cold running water. Drain. Mix with sesame seed oil. Set aside.

2. Cut pork crosswise and julienne. Mix with 1 tablespoon of light soy sauce and cornstarch. Stir-fry scallion and pork in 2 tablespoons heated oil until meat changes color. Add 1 tablespoon light soy sauce and sugar. Remove. Keep pork warm.

3. In clean wok, stir-fry cabbage in 2 tablespoons heated oil 2 minutes. Remove. Wipe out wok.

4. Heat 3 tablespoons of oil in wok. Add noodles. Do not stir. Let noodles brown on bottom (about 5 minutes). Turn noodle cake over. Brown other side in same manner. Remove to warm platter.

5. Heat 1 tablespoon of oil in wok. Add pork and cabbage. Add dark soy sauce. Stir-fry until thoroughly heated. Thicken with dissolved cornstarch. Pour over noodles. Wipe out wok.

6. Heat 1 tablespoon oil to smoking hot in wok. Wilt spinach. Add salt. Stir-fry quickly 10 seconds.

7. Arrange spinach around mound of covered noodles. Serve with red wine vinegar.

May be prepared in advance through step 2, with vegetables cut up. Do not freeze.

Serves 4 to 6

Snow Cabbage Noodles   SHANGHAI

Pickled snow cabbage has a distinctive flavor; it goes well with any meat. In China it is made with mustard greens and is pickled in extremely cold weather. Thus the name "snow."

½ pound shredded pork
1 teaspoon salt
½ teaspoon cornstarch
3½ tablespoons plus ½ teaspoon oil
1½ teaspoons sherry
3 ounces pickled snow cabbage

½ teaspoon sugar
½ pound Chinese fresh water
  noodles (medium)
¼ cup cold water
6 cups chicken stock

1. Mix pork with ½ teaspoon of salt, cornstarch, and ½ teaspoon of oil.
2. Heat 2 tablespoons of oil in wok. Stir-fry pork until color changes. Add sherry. Cook 1 minute. Remove to plate.
3. Heat 1½ tablespoons of oil in wok. Stir-fry snow cabbage 1 minute. Add pork mixture. Stir-fry 1 minute. Add sugar. Stir-fry 1 second. Remove to plate.
4. Drop noodles into boiling water to cover. Cook 4 minutes. When water boils, add ¼ cup cold water. Bring to boil again. Drain. Remove.
5. Bring stock to boil. Add remaining ½ teaspoon salt.
6. Add noodles to boiling stock. Bring to boil again.
7. Remove noodles to tureen. Pour in stock. Place cabbage mixture on top.

May be prepared in advance through step 1. Do not freeze.

Serves 4 to 6

Tai Tai Mein   SZECHWAN

If you like spicy dishes, famous Tai Tai Mein is pleasing and simple to prepare.

2 tablespoons light soy sauce
4½ teaspoons sesame seed oil
1½ teaspoons red wine vinegar
1 clove garlic, chopped fine
1½ teaspoons chili paste
    with garlic
2 tablespoons chicken stock
½ pound Chinese fresh-water
    noodles (fine)

Boiling water
2 tablespoons Szechwan preserved
    vegetable, chopped fine
2 tablespoons roasted peanuts,
    chopped fine
1 scallion, chopped fine
Peppercorn salt (optional)

1. Combine soy sauce, 1½ teaspoons sesame seed oil, red wine vinegar, garlic, chili paste with garlic, and stock in a bowl. Stir well. Set aside.
2. Put noodles into boiling water 5 minutes. Stir constantly. Drain. Mix with 3 teaspoons sesame seed oil.
3. Put noodles into bowl. Pour sauce over them. Sprinkle preserved vegetable, peanuts, and scallions on top. Add a little peppercorn salt, if desired.

May be prepared in advance through step 1. Do not freeze.

Serves 4 to 6

Faults are big when love is small.

Three-Flavored Lo Mein   YANGCHOW

Noodles are always a welcome dish on the table. This is another one-dish meal—noodles with three meat ingredients and crunchy vegetables.

¼ pound bok choy (Chinese green)
1 pound Chinese fresh-water
    noodles (medium)
1 tablespoon oil
4 ounces flank steak, shredded
4 ounces fresh shrimp, shelled,
    deveined, cut in halves
4 ounces chicken, sliced thin
1 egg white
1 teaspoon salt
1 tablespoon cornstarch

4 cups oil for deep frying
¼ cup bamboo shoots, shredded
4 tablespoons light soy sauce
½ pound bean sprouts
4 dried black mushrooms
    (soaked in boiling water 20
    minutes, cooked 20 minutes,
    stems removed, shredded)
2 tablespoons sesame seed oil
¼ cup chicken stock

1. Wash bok choy. Drain. Discard outer leaves. Cut into 1½-inch pieces.
2. Boil noodles in 8 cups water 4 minutes. Drain. Rinse under cold water.
Toss with 1 tablespoon oil. Set aside.
3. Combine steak, shrimp, and chicken with egg white, salt, and cornstarch.
Mix well with hand.
4. Heat oil until very hot. Deep fry meat mixture 1 minute. Drain.
Remove.
5. Reheat 2 tablespoons of oil in wok. Stir-fry bok choy and bamboo
shoots 1 minute. Add meat mixture and 1 tablespoon of soy sauce. Stir-fry
30 seconds. Add bean sprouts and mushrooms. Stir-fry 1 minute more.
Remove meat and vegetable mixture to bowl. Reserve drippings in wok.
6. In wok combine noodles, 3 tablespoons soy sauce, sesame seed oil, and
stock. Stir over moderate heat until thoroughly hot. Remove to large
platter. Pour meat and vegetable mixture over top. Toss.

May be prepared in advance through step 3. Do not freeze.

Serves 4 to 6

Rice

Rice is the staple food of China. It is served for breakfast, lunch, and dinner, to the very old and to the very young. Rice sustains the poor, succors the rich, nourishes the invalids, and is the privilege of any beggar.

A child must eat every grain in his rice bowl and is taught early to appreciate the hard life of the laborer in the rice fields.

The word rice has many connotations. It is usual to say, "Have you had rice?" meaning, "Have you eaten or had dinner?"

"I lost my rice bowl" means "I lost my job."

To throw a rice bowl on the floor is meant as a great insult, a gesture of anger and contempt.

Basic Rice Recipe ALL REGIONS

People ask me why my rice is so fluffy. Here is the secret. It is the old method of cooking rice. No matter what amount of rice you cook, here is the direct way.

2 cups long-grain rice
Water

1. Wash rice with hands 5 times until water is clear. Pour into saucepan.
2. Now, measure with your index finger to see if the water is one knuckle above the rice (1 inch). This is the exact amount of water that is needed.
3. Bring rice to boil. Let cook until all of the water is evaporated (about 4 minutes).
4. Cover. Simmer 30 minutes.

Serves 4 to 6

Chicken with Rice   CANTON

This is another healthy, one-dish meal.

2 cups long-grain rice
1 pound boneless and skinless
    chicken breast, cut into
    1-inch pieces
1 teaspoon salt
1 teaspoon cornstarch
3 tablespoons oil
1 slice ginger, chopped fine

1 scallion, chopped fine
4 dried black mushrooms (soaked
    in boiling water 20 minutes,
    stems removed, halved)
1 tablespoon sherry
2 tablespoons dark soy sauce
¼ teaspoon sugar

1. Wash rice thoroughly in cold water. Cover with water until it is 1 inch above rice. Set aside.
2. Mix chicken with salt, cornstarch, and 1 tablespoon of oil in bowl.
3. Heat 2 tablespoons of oil in wok. Stir-fry ginger and scallion 30 seconds. Pour in chicken. Stir-fry 1 minute. Add mushrooms, sherry, soy sauce, and sugar. Stir-fry thoroughly 1 minute. Set aside.
4. Bring rice to boil over high heat. Boil until water is evaporated. Turn to low heat.
5. Quickly spread chicken mixture on top of rice. Cover and cook 20 to 25 minutes on low heat.
6. Toss chicken ingredients with rice before serving.

May be prepared in advance through step 5 or frozen after step 6.

Serves 4 to 6

Curry Beef Fried Rice   CANTON

We Chinese appear to have endless ways to prepare rice. Here is one with flavoring borrowed from India.

4 tablespoons oil	**4 cups cold, cooked rice**
½ onion, chopped fine	**1 teaspoon salt**
½ pound ground beef	**1 scallion, chopped fine**
1 tablespoon curry powder	

1. Heat oil in wok. Stir-fry onion until light brown. Add beef. Stir-fry on high heat 1 minute.
2. Add curry powder. Stir-fry on moderate heat until there is an aroma. Add rice and salt. Stir-fry until thoroughly heated.
3. Add scallion. Stir-fry about 30 seconds more.

May be prepared in advance through step 2 or frozen after step 3.

Serves 4 to 6

Don't promise easily; once you promise, do it and keep it.

Curry Chicken Rice   CANTON

Here is another Indian-influenced dish. This one is a delicious casserole.

2 cups long grain rice	**4 tablespoons oil**
1 pound boneless, skinless	**½ onion, sliced**
chicken breast, cut into	**2 tablespoons curry paste**
1-inch pieces	**1 tablespoon sherry**
1 teaspoon salt	
1 teaspoon cornstarch	

1. Wash rice and rinse thoroughly in cold water. Cover with water to reach 1 inch above rice. Bring rice to boil over high heat. Boil until water is evaporated. Turn heat to low.
2. Mix chicken with salt, cornstarch, and 1½ teaspoons of oil.
3. Heat 1½ teaspoons of oil in wok. Stir-fry onion 1 minute. Remove. Set aside.
4. Heat 3 tablespoons oil in wok. Pour in curry paste. Stir-fry on low heat 1 minute.
5. Turn to high heat. Pour in chicken. Stir-fry 1 minute. Add onion and sherry. Stir-fry thoroughly 1 minute.
6. Quickly pour curried chicken mixture on top of rice. Cover and cook 20 minutes.
7. Toss curried mixture with rice before serving.

May be prepared in advance through step 6 or frozen after step 7.

Serves 4 to 6

Plain Fried Rice   ALL REGIONS

The Chinese do not fry rice with soy sauce—this combination has more appeal to Westerners. Actually, fried rice is a dish of leftovers. The rice has been cooked and any meat or vegetable can be added. (See next two recipes.)

4 cups cold cooked rice	1 teaspoon salt
4 tablespoons oil	Pepper to taste
3 beaten eggs	1 scallion, chopped fine

1. Break rice apart with wet hands.
2. Heat oil on high flame in wok. Stir-fry rice rapidly, turning spatula constantly until rice is thoroughly heated.
3. Make a well in center of rice. Pour in beaten eggs. Stir eggs until they are scrambled. Then stir-fry eggs into the rice until thoroughly blended. Add salt and pepper. Stir-fry 30 seconds. Add scallion.

May be prepared in advance. May be frozen. Reheat before serving.

Serves 4 to 6

Pork Fried Rice   CANTON

This is a fine way to use leftover rice.

4 tablespoons oil	2 tablespoons dark soy sauce
2 beaten eggs	1 cup roast pork, diced small
4 cups cold cooked rice	2 scallions, chopped fine
½ teaspoon salt	

1. Heat 2 tablespoons of oil in wok. Scramble beaten eggs. Remove. Set aside.
2. Heat 2 tablespoons oil in wok. Stir-fry rice on high heat breaking up lumps by pressing rice against the pan, turning quickly and constantly.
3. Add salt, soy sauce, pork, scallions, and scrambled eggs. Stir-fry to heat thoroughly.

May be prepared in advance. May be frozen. Reheat before serving.

Serves 4 to 6

Shrimp Fried Rice   ALL REGIONS

This is yet another great dish with leftover rice.

½ pound fresh shrimp, shelled and deveined	5 tablespoons oil
1 teaspoon cornstarch	3 beaten eggs
½ teaspoon salt	4 cups cold cooked rice
	2 tablespoons light soy sauce
	1 scallion, chopped fine

1. Cut shrimp into small pieces. Mix with cornstarch and salt.
2. Heat 1 tablespoon of oil in wok. Stir-fry shrimp until pink, about 30 seconds. Remove.
3. Heat 2 tablespoons of oil in wok. Pour in beaten eggs. Scramble fine. Remove.
4. Heat 2 tablespoons oil in wok. Add rice and soy sauce. Stir-fry until thoroughly heated. Add scrambled eggs, shrimp, and scallion. Stir-fry 30 seconds.

May be prepared in advance. May be frozen. Reheat before serving.

Serves 4 to 6

Seafood Rice

CANTON

This is an easy, elegant one-dish meal.

3 eggs
1½ teaspoons salt
7 tablespoons oil
1 scallion, chopped fine
½ cup fresh shrimp, shelled,
    deveined, cut into cubes
1 teaspoon cornstarch
3 cups cooked rice

1½ cups chicken stock
2 tablespoons cornstarch,
    dissolved in 2 tablespoons
    water
½ cup crab meat
½ cup cooked lobster meat,
    cut into cubes
1 tablespoon sherry
Pinch of pepper

1. Beat eggs slightly with ½ teaspoon of salt.
2. Heat 2 tablespoons of oil in wok. Add scallion. Pour in eggs and scramble until set. Remove to plate.
3. Mix shrimp with cornstarch and ½ teaspoon salt. Heat 1 tablespoon oil in wok. Stir-fry shrimp until pink, about 30 seconds. Remove to plate.
4. Heat 2 tablespoons of oil in wok. Stir-fry rice over moderate heat until thoroughly heated. Add ½ teaspoon salt. Pour in scrambled eggs. Stir-fry mixture 1 minute. Remove to greased casserole dish.
5. Heat 2 tablespoons oil in wok. Pour in stock. Thicken with dissolved cornstarch. Add shrimp, crab meat, and lobster. Bring to boil. Add sherry and pepper.
6. Pour seafood mixture over rice mixture.
7. Bake uncovered at 400 degrees 10 minutes.

May be prepared in advance through step 6. Before serving, bake 20 minutes. Do not freeze.

Serves 4 to 6

The glory of life is being useful.

Rice Crispy Snack   PEKING

Have you heard of sizzling rice? It is the crust that sticks to the bottom of the pan after boiling. Deep-fry it and make a delicious snack by sprinkling salt and sugar on top—or drop it into soup.

2 cups long grain rice   Salt to taste
2 to 4 cups oil for deep-frying   Sugar to taste

1. Wash rice thoroughly in pot. Cover with cold water 1 inch above it.
2. Cover pot. Bring to boil. Simmer over low heat 30 minutes.
3. Remove all soft rice, leaving only the crust at the bottom and sides of the pan. (Soft rice can be used for any fried rice dish.)
4. Brown crust over low heat 1 hour, uncovered. Cool.
5. Remove crust from pot. Break into pieces.
6. Deep-fry crust. Season with salt and sugar. Store in can.

May be prepared in advance. Do not freeze.

Serves 4 to 6

Sun Ya Fried Rice   CANTON

Once in Shanghai there was a famous restaurant called Sun Ya. This was one of its most popular dishes. It goes well with Empress Chicken.

6 tablespoons oil
2 eggs, beaten with ½ teaspoon
    salt
½ cup fresh shrimp, shelled,
    deveined, and washed
1½ teaspoons sherry
4 cups cold cooked rice
½ teaspoon salt

½ cup cooked chicken, diced
¼ cup roast pork*
2 dried black mushrooms, (soaked
    in boiling water 20 minutes,
    stems removed, cooked 20
    minutes), diced
2 tablespoons chicken stock
2 tablespoons frozen peas, blanched
    1 minute in boiling water
    and rinsed under cold water

1. Heat 2 tablespoons of oil in wok. When very hot, pour in beaten eggs and scramble briskly with spoon. Set aside.

2. Heat 2 tablespoons of oil in wok. Stir-fry shrimp on high heat 30 seconds. Add sherry. Stir-fry 10 seconds. Remove to plate. Set aside.
3. Heat 2 tablespoons of oil in wok. Add rice. Stir constantly over moderate heat, breaking up the lumps with spoon. Add salt.
4. Continue stirring until rice becomes hot. Pour in chicken, pork, mushrooms, and scrambled eggs. Stir-fry to mix. Add stock to moisten scrambled ingredients.
5. Add shrimp and peas. Stir-fry until thoroughly heated and mixed.

---

* This is a very flexible recipe. You may vary it with leftover turkey, duck, or lobster.

Chicken, pork, rice, shrimp, and mushrooms may be prepared in advance and meats may be frozen. Thaw and proceed with step 1.

Serves 4 to 6

Vegetable Rice   ALL REGIONS

Here is an ideal dish for vegetarians!

2 cups rice
4 tablespoons oil
1 pound bok choy (Chinese green), cleaned and cut into 1-inch pieces
1½ teaspoons salt

4 dried black mushrooms (soaked in boiling water 20 minutes, stems removed) diced
1 tablespoon light soy sauce

1. Wash rice thoroughly in cold water. Place in pot and cover with water 1 inch above rice.
2. Heat 4 tablespoons oil in wok. Stir-fry bok choy on high heat. Add salt and mushrooms. Stir-fry 2 minutes.
3. Bring rice to boil. Add vegetables and soy sauce to top of rice. Cover. Cook on low heat 30 minutes.
4. Toss vegetables with rice thoroughly before serving.

May be prepared in advance. May be frozen. Steam before serving.

Serves 4 to 6

Congees (Porridge)

Congee is rice cooked with large amounts of water or chicken stock. It is good for convalescents, as it is meant for a tired stomach. The Chinese eat congee for breakfast and supper. It can be accompanied by eggs, pickled vegetables, salted peanuts, fish, or ham.

There was a traditional congee in our family. Every eighth day of the twelfth month, in the extreme cold of December, we served this special congee called "La Pa." (La means extreme cold month, Pa means eight.) We prepared this congee with eight ingredients—red dates, fresh water chestnuts, soybeans, bok choy, fresh chestnuts, ham, and chicken. What a highly nourishing congee! Even the tired, worn-out hunter was refreshed by it, and the children were thrilled when they ate it.

La Pa Congee

This is the congee my family has served for more than one hundred years.

2 cups long grain rice
16 cups water
2 tablespoons oil
1 pound bok choy (Chinese green), cut into 1-inch pieces
12 fresh water chestnuts, skin on
¼ cup soy beans, soaked in water overnight
10 red dates or ¼ cup skinless peanuts
10 fresh chestnuts, blanched, peeled, and halved

1 whole chicken breast, boned, skinned, and diced
¼ cup (cooked) Virginia ham, diced
2 teaspoons salt
10 dried black mushrooms, soaked overnight, stems removed, halved
Salt to taste

1. Wash rice thoroughly and place in pot. Add water and bring to boil. Simmer 30 minutes.
2. Heat oil in wok. Stir-fry bok choy 1 minute and remove.
3. Add bok choy, fresh water chestnuts, soy beans, red dates or peanuts, fresh chestnuts, and mushrooms to rice. Bring to boil. Simmer 30 minutes.
4. Add ham and chicken. Cook 10 minutes. Stir gently occasionally. Season with salt to taste.

May be prepared in advance. May be frozen.

Serves 8

Fish Congee

ALL REGIONS

For me, this is a complete and satisfying meal, healthful and not too filling. If you like, serve with Cold Asparagus Salad.

1 cup long-grain rice	2 teaspoons salt
12 cups water or chicken stock	1 cup lettuce, shredded (optional)
½ pound fish fillet, sliced	1 scallion, shredded
very thin	1 slice ginger, finely shredded
1 tablespoon light soy sauce	Pepper to taste
2 tablespoons oil	1 tablespoon sesame seed oil

1. Wash rice thoroughly. Put in pot. Add water or stock. Bring to boil. Simmer over low flame 3 hours until rice and liquid become like thin paste.
2. Mix fish with soy sauce and 1 tablespoon of oil. Set aside.
3. Add salt and lettuce to rice after it has finished cooking. Stir gently in one direction. Cook 1 minute.
4. Add seasoned fish, scallion, ginger, and 1 tablespoon oil. Bring to boil. Turn off heat.
5. Sprinkle with pepper and whirl sesame seed oil on top.
6. Serve hot in individual small bowls.

May be prepared in advance through step 1. Do not freeze.

Serves 4 to 6

Vegetable Congee   ALL REGIONS

To this congee you can add soybeans, ginkgo nuts, lotus seeds, sweet potatoes, carrots, peas, zucchini, string beans, or any other vegetable that pleases you.

1 cup long-grain rice
10 cups water
4 tablespoons oil
1 pound bok choy (Chinese green),
     diced

3 teaspoons salt
6 dried black mushrooms soaked
     in boiling water 20 minutes,
     stems removed, diced

1. Wash rice thoroughly.
2. Pour water into pot. Add rice. Bring to boil.
3. Meanwhile, heat oil in wok. Stir-fry bok choy 1 minute. Add 1 teaspoon of salt.
4. Pour bok choy and mushrooms into rice. Add 2 teaspoons salt.
5. Cover and simmer 2 hours.

May be prepared in advance. May be frozen. Reheat before serving.

Serves 4 to 6

Lotus comes up from the mud.

12

Desserts

Compared to the great variety of other dishes the Chinese have, there are few sweet ones. I believe American doctors now are substantiating the Chinese way regarding sweets. Recent studies show that chocolate and rich pastries contain a great deal of cholesterol and fats—they are bad for the heart as well as the teeth.

In China, children are taught at an early age that candy is bad for the teeth. However, they love fruit. Fruit is healthy and an aid to digestion after meals. I prefer fruit as a finale to my own dinner parties.

The seasons in China produce different fruits. We love them from distant places—the lychee from Canton, the crunchy pear from Tientsin, the peach from Funghwa, Chekiang.

A story comes to mind of an Emperor of the Tang Dynasty in the eighth century. His concubine, Yang Kwei Fei, had a great passion for lychees. Each day, at great expense, he sent his carrier on horseback for the express purpose of getting the best and freshest lychees for her. This was too extravagant for his people. Because of this, they rebelled. In all of China's history, he was the only emperor to lose his throne!

Almond Delight   PEKING

This is a soothing, cooling, refreshing dessert for any season. It can be served with canned or fresh fruits.

1 package unflavored gelatin	*Syrup*
1½ cups cold water	
¼ cup sugar	**1½ cups water**
1 can evaporated milk	**½ cup sugar**
2 teaspoons almond extract	**1 teaspoon almond extract**
	1 can fruit cocktail or fresh
	fruits

1. Dissolve gelatin in ¼ cup of cold water. Set aside 10 minutes.
2. Heat 1¼ cups water in saucepan. Add sugar. Bring to boil. Turn off heat. Add milk. Stir well. Pour this liquid into gelatin mixture. Add almond extract. Stir well.
3. Pour ingredients into an oblong 8″ x 8″ x 2″ Pyrex dish. Allow to set. Chill in refrigerator.
4. To make syrup: Pour water and sugar into saucepan. Bring to boil. Cool. Add almond extract. Stir well. Chill.
5. Cut jellied mixture into diamond shapes. Serve cold with fruit cocktail or diced fresh fruits and chilled syrup.

May be prepared in advance and refrigerated. Do not freeze.

Serves 4 to 6

You must be serene when you cook Chinese.

Chinese Crullers
(Fried Devils)

ALL REGIONS

The name "Fried Devils" is derived from a story steeped in Confucian tradition. The tale is about a traitor, Chin Kuei, who betrayed a hero, Yueh Fei. Yueh Fei was a famous scholar, poet, and general during the Sung dynasty. Chin Kuei, who was a government minister, and his wife formed an alliance with the Mongolian tribes and had Yueh Fei falsely accused of treason and put to death. To remind posterity that a traitor will never be forgiven, the Chinese named this dish "Yu Za Kuei," which literally means "deep fried devils." Whenever the dish is eaten, traitors Chin Kuei and his evil wife are fried in oil for eternity!

1 teaspoon salt	⅞ cup water
¾ teaspoon alum	2 cups all-purpose flour
1 teaspoon baking soda	8 cups oil for deep-frying
¾ teaspoon ammonium bicarbonate	

1. Place salt, alum, baking soda, and ammonium bicarbonate in mixing bowl. Add water and stir until thoroughly dissolved. Add flour. Stir with chopstick to make soft, smooth dough.
2. Knead dough until it is elastic. Cover and let stand at least 4 hours.
3. Remove dough and stretch it into a long strip, ⅓-inch thick and 2 inches wide. Sprinkle with a little flour.
4. Using a knife or cleaver, cut dough into 20 strips ½-inch wide.
5. Pick up a strip from the end with spatula, turn it around and place directly on top of next strip (10 pieces).
6. Lay a chopstick on top of these double strips. Press down. Repeat process with remaining pieces.
7. Heat oil for deep-frying. Pick up one double strip. Hold the two ends and stretch it until it is 9 inches long.
8. Drop into hot oil. Turn dough on both sides continuously with chopstick until it is golden brown and expands. Remove and drain. Repeat with other strips.

May be prepared in advance and refrigerated or frozen. Before serving, thaw, if necessary, and reheat in oven at 400 degrees for five minutes.

10 Crullers

Eight Precious Pudding   SHANGHAI

This is a famous traditional banquet dessert. Usually it contains eight kinds of dried candied fruits that represent eight precious stones. The combination of sweet rice and bean paste gives it an exquisite taste.

1 ounce lotus seeds	3 tablespoons oil
2 cups cold water	1 red maraschino cherry, stemless
2 ounces Chinese red dates	1 cup any candied fruits
2 cups glutinous rice	1 cup red bean paste
¼ cup sugar	

1. Add lotus seeds to cold water in saucepan. Bring to boil. Simmer on low heat 20 minutes. Drain and cool. Split into halves. Set aside.
2. Put red dates in bowl on rack in pot or in steamer. Steam covered over boiling water 30 minutes. Set aside.
3. Put rice in pot with water level ¾-inch above rice. Bring to boil. Simmer 20 minutes. Stir in sugar and remaining 2 tablespoons oil. Mix well. Set aside.
4. Grease medium-sized bowl heavily with oil. Place cherry in center. Arrange lotus seeds, red dates, and candied fruits in circles around bottom and up to edge of bowl, glazed side down.
5. Spread a layer of rice mixture over fruits carefully so as not to spoil the design.
6. Spoon a layer of red bean paste over the rice. Cover with another layer of rice. Pack tight.
7. Place bowl on rack in pot or in steamer. Cover. Steam over boiling water 1 hour.
8. Remove pudding carefully by running flexible spatula around edge. Put serving plate over bowl and invert bowl. Serve pudding with Sweet Almond Sauce.

May be prepared in advance through step 7. May be frozen after step 7. Resteam before serving.

Serves 4 to 6

Sweet Almond Sauce

3 tablespoons sugar
1 cup water

1 teaspoon almond extract
1 tablespoon cornstarch dissolved
    in 2 tablespoons water

Boil sugar and water. Add almond extract. Thicken with dissolved cornstarch.

Preserved Kumquats   ALL REGIONS

A light dessert—and this one is so easy to prepare.

1 pound fresh kumquats
2 cups sugar
1 cup water

1. Wash kumquats. Put a slit in each end so they will not burst while cooking.
2. Bring sugar and water to boil. Simmer covered about 10 minutes.
3. Add kumquats. Cook 30 minutes or until tender. Will keep in jar in refrigerator indefinitely.

May be prepared in advance. May be frozen.

Serves 6

Your best helper is yourself.

Red Bean Paste   ALL REGIONS

Beans contain protein and also are rich in vitamin B. This paste is a filling for steamed buns or pastries.

1 pound Chinese red beans
2 tablespoons oil
½ pound sugar

1. Soak beans in water to cover overnight.
2. Boil beans in water to cover. Simmer covered 1 hour over low heat until soft.
3. Pour beans into strainer and place strainer in large basin filled with cold water.
4. Use hand or spoon to rub beans against the strainer, which will remove husks and permit mashed bean paste to pass through into the basin of water.
5. Pour water and mashed bean paste into a cloth bag (5 pound rice bag may be used). Squeeze dry. Remove paste from bag.
6. Heat oil in wok. Add bean paste. Stir-fry constantly until it becomes darker. Add sugar. Stir and cook on low heat 5 minutes.

May be prepared in advance. May be frozen.

Red-in-Snow Mousse   SHANGHAI

This is a Western dessert, turned Chinese with crab apple sauce by the proprietor of Sun Ya restaurant in Shanghai 50 years ago. As red is the color that gladdens the heart of any Oriental, it has become a most popular dessert.

1 package unflavored gelatin	**1½ cups boiling water**
½ cup cold water	**½ pint whipping cream**
⅔ cup sugar	**Crab apple or whole cranberry sauce**

1. Dissolve gelatin in ½ cup cold water. Set aside 5 minutes.
2. Pour sugar into boiling water. Bring to boil. Add gelatin mixture. Boil 1 minute. Remove. Cool ingredients until they are about to set.
3. Whip cream until stiff. Fold lightly into gelatin mixture.
4. Pour mixture into a ring mold that has been rinsed in cold water. Chill it thoroughly.
5. Unmold and serve with crab apple sauce or whole cranberry sauce in center.

May be prepared in advance through step 3. May be frozen after step 3.

Crab Apple Sauce

1 pound crab apples	**2 cups water**
Boiling water	**1¼ cups sugar**

1. Wash crab apples. Cut into halves crosswise. Remove seeds. Plunge them into boiling water. Drain. Peel.
2. Combine seeds and skins in saucepan with 2 cups water. Boil 2 minutes. Strain liquid. Reserve.
3. Combine crab apple liquid and sugar in saucepan. Cook 2 minutes. Add crab apples and cook 8 minutes. Cool. Serve inside Red-In-Snow Mousse (mold).

NOTE: If crab apples are not available, serve whole cranberry sauce.

Serves 6

Rice Wine   ALL REGIONS

Rice wine is an interesting dessert, yet we use it as a cooking ingredient in place of sherry. It gives a marvelous flavor to fish and seafood, especially in Szechwan dishes.

3 cups sweet rice	**1 tablespoon flour**
1 wine ball	**½ cup cold water**

1. Wash rice thoroughly. Cover with cold water. Soak overnight.
2. Mash wine ball into powder with rolling pin between 2 sheets of aluminum foil. Add flour. Mix well with finger. Set aside.
3. Line steamer rack with wet cloth. Spread rice evenly on cloth. Steam rice over boiling water 20 minutes.
4. Remove rice to a strainer. Rinse with cold water. Then rinse with warm water (about 80 degrees). Drain.
5. Rinse an earthenware pot or casserole with warm water. Put in rice. Add wine powder. Use hands to gently mix well. Smooth down the rice with palm of hand. Make a 1-inch hole in center floor of pot. Pour ½ cup cold water into hole. Cover.
6. Wrap earthenware pot in a blanket, covering it entirely.
7. Leave in a dark place 24 hours. By this time a sweet-flavored liquid will appear in center and also at the sides. This is the wine.
8. Remove rice wine to tightly covered bottles. It will keep indefinitely refrigerated.
9. Serve hot or cold. May be used as a substitute for sherry in Szechwan dishes.

May be prepared in advance through step 8. Do not freeze.

Serves 4 to 6

Sesame Seed Fried Custard   YANGCHOW

It is impossible to describe the fantastic delicacy of this custard. It is as light as a puff of summer air!

½ cup sesame seeds	3 eggs, beaten
¼ cup powdered sugar	1 teaspoon vanilla
1 cup flour	¼ cup cornstarch
2 tablespoons granulated sugar	2 to 4 cups oil for deep-frying
1½ cups water	

1. Toast sesame seeds in dry pan in 300-degree oven until light brown, about 20 minutes. Cool. Mix with powdered sugar. Set aside.
2. Mix flour with granulated sugar in bowl. Stir in ½ cup of water. Add beaten eggs. Mix until smooth.
3. Pour 1 cup water into saucepan. Bring to boil. Add flour mixture. Stir vigorously over moderate heat until it thickens. Add vanilla. Stir well.
4. Pour mixture into greased 8-inch-square Pyrex dish. Pat with hand to ½-inch thickness. Cool in refrigerator.
5. Cut in strips 1½-inches long and ½-inch wide. Dredge strips with cornstarch.
6. Heat oil to moderately hot. Fry strips, a few at a time, 3 minutes or until light brown. Lift out with strainer as soon as they get brown. Remove to serving plate.
7. Sprinkle with sesame seed mixture. Serve hot.

May be prepared in advance through step 5. May be frozen after step 5.

Serves 6

The banquet must end; the child must be weaned. I am so sad when I must say goodbye to my students.

Steamed Apples   PEKING

I come from a family of doctors: therefore, I know a little bit about medicine. Apples contain pectin and vitamins, both of which purify the blood. In fact, my grandfather, whose books are still used as medical texts in China, prescribed an apple a day for his patients as preventive medicine as far back as the 19th century.

6 apples
6 tablespoons Red Bean Paste

½ cup whipping cream
2 tablespoons sugar
½ teaspoon vanilla

1. Core apples, being careful not to cut through to bottom.
2. Fill each apple with 1 tablespoon Red Bean Paste.
3. Put apples upright on a plate. Place plate on rack in pot or in steamer. Steam covered over boiling water 30 minutes.
4. Whip cream, adding sugar and vanilla until stiff. Decorate top of apples with whipped cream. If you wish to be fancy, squeeze whipped cream through a pastry bag, making a rose pattern on top of each.

Do not prepare in advance. Do not freeze.

6 apples

Steamed Pears   PEKING

Pears are a popular Chinese dessert. They are good for colds and coughs and are soothing to the throat. This fruit is said to stop aging and keep you young. It is advisable for those with high blood pressure to eat pears often.

6 pears
6 tablespoons honey

1. Cut 1 inch from top of each pear. Reserve tops for lids. Core each pear—do no make hole in bottom.
2. Fill pears with honey. Replace lids.
3. Place pears upright on plate. Place plate on rack in pot or in steamer. Steam covered over boiling water 30 minutes. Serve hot.

May be prepared in advance through step 2. Do not freeze.

Serves 6

Peking Wall   PEKING

This "wall" is a thing of beauty, not only to see but to taste, as well. This dessert was served in the palace at the end of the Ching Dynasty to ambassadors of foreign countries.

1 pound fresh chestnuts	2 fresh mandarin oranges
3 tablespoons powdered sugar	½ cup pitted dates
1 pound granulated sugar	10 fresh strawberries
1 cup water	½ pint whipping cream
½ cup walnut halves	1 teaspoon vanilla

1. Cut chestnuts in half. Boil in water to cover 30 minutes. Cool and peel. Mash chestnuts in a strainer over a mixing bowl. Press them through the strainer until pureed. This is the Peking "dust."
2. Mix powdered sugar lightly with dust. Set aside.
3. Boil 1 cup of sugar with ½ cup of water in an immaculately clean pan until crystallized or until it spins. Keep crystallized sugar over very low heat.
4. Dip walnuts, oranges, dates, and strawberries one by one in crystallized sugar. Put them on a greased plate.
5. On a serving plate cement walnuts, oranges, dates, and strawberries with a little additional crystallized sugar; making four joined "walls" in a square shape. Put one piece on top of another until "walls" are 4 inches high.
6. Whip cream until soft. Add 3 tablespoons sugar and vanilla. Continue to whip until stiff.
7. Put dust inside walls. Garnish walls with whipping cream inside and out with rose pattern (use pastry bag).
8. Keep crystallized sugar over low heat. If there is none left, repeat step 3.
9. Place ends of two long chopsticks 6 inches apart on a table so that they jut out at least 1 foot.
10. Dip another pair of chopsticks into crystallized sugar. As you pull the sugar, you will form threads. Spin threads on the two long chopsticks in circular motion. When there is a pile of spun sugar, take it from the sticks and place it on the wall.

May be prepared in advance through step 2. Do not freeze.

Serves 6

13

Teas

As rice is the staple food of China, tea is the staple beverage. Infants are weaned on it, and a folk saying goes, "I need some tea to cheer my old age."

The earliest recorded reference to tea is in a letter written in 317 A.D. by Liu Kun, a Chinese military leader, to his nephew.

The first book about tea, published in the year 780 by Lu Yu, suggests: "When feeling hot, thirsty, depressed, suffering from headache, fatigue of the four limbs or pains in the joints, one should drink tea only. The beverage is like dark red wine and sweet dew."

Lin Yutang, the Chinese philosopher, wrote that "Tea is symbolic of earthly purity, requiring the most fastidious cleanliness in its preparation from picking, drying, and preserving to its final infusion and drinking."

There are three basic kinds of Chinese tea:

1. Green: Unfermented Tea
    Dragon Well—most famous.
    Gunpowder—from North China.
    Lu An—from Anhwei Province.
    Water Nymph—scented with narcissus.

2. Oolong: Semifermented Tea
    Jasmine (scented)
    Chrysanthemum (scented)
    Lo Cha—from Formosa
    Oolong—from Formosa
3. Black: Fermented Tea
    Black Dragon—from Kwangtung
    Iron Goddess of Mercy—from Fukien
    Keemun—most famous, from Anhwei
    Lychee Tea (scented)
    Rose Tea with Dried Rosebud (scented)
    Puer—from Yunnan

HOW TO MAKE GOOD TEA:

1. Tea pots made of glass, china, or earthenware are best. *Never* use a metal pot.
2. Use one teaspoon tea (or one tea bag) for each cup of water, plus one for the pot.
3. Pour boiling water onto tea leaves.
4. Steep from 3 to 5 minutes.
5. After steeping, the tea should be strained off into another heated pot or the tea bags removed.

14

Sauces and Dips

Life is uneven and full of changes. In our journey of life, we often encounter experiences that might be called "sweet," "sour," "bitter," and "spicy." Taking a philosophical attitude toward life as well as food, the Chinese chef divides the seasonings of sauces into four categories, representing the tastes of life. For instance, sweet sour sauce is used for fried fish, pork, and shrimp. Bitterness is an ingredient to be avoided in life—hence, there is no special bitter sauce in Chinese cuisine. Spicy sauces are prepared from hot mustard and red chili peppers and are especially suitable as dips. Other Chinese sauces include soy sauce, bean sauce, and hoisin sauce, widely used in Chinese dishes. Another interesting sauce is the Master Marinade, (see Thousand Year Sauce Chicken), used for meat and poultry.

Bean Sauce I   ALL REGIONS

1 tablespoon oil   ¼ cup water
2 tablespoons bean sauce   1 teaspoon sesame seed oil
2 tablespoons sugar

1. Heat oil in wok. Add bean sauce. Stir over low heat 2 minutes.
2. Add sugar and water. Stir 30 seconds. Add sesame seed oil. Stir well.

NOTE: Use on Chinese Pancakes and steamed buns.

May be prepared in advance, bottled and refrigerated indefinitely. Do not freeze.

Bean Sauce II   ALL REGIONS

¼ cup hoisin sauce   2 teaspoons sugar
2 tablespoons water   1½ teaspoons sesame seed oil

Combine all ingredients in wok. Stir 1 minute.

NOTE: Use as Bean Sauce I.

Peppercorn Salt

2 tablespoons Chinese peppercorns
¼ cup salt

1. Brown peppercorns and salt in dry frying pan over low heat until fragrance comes out.
2. Place a piece of foil on a flat surface. Pour mixture onto foil. Fold foil over. Crush with rolling pin. Strain. May be stored indefinitely in a jar on pantry shelf.

NOTE: Use as seasoning or as a dip.

Sweet Sour Sauce

¼ cup catsup
¼ cup sugar
1 cup water
¼ cup white vinegar

2 heaping tablespoons cornstarch,
   dissolved in 2 tablespoons
   water
1 green pepper, cut into squares
2 tablespoons canned pineapple
   chunks

1. Combine first 4 ingredients in saucepan. Bring to boil.
2. Thicken with dissolved cornstarch. Stir constantly.
3. Add green pepper and pineapple. Stir.

NOTE: Use as a dip.

May be refrigerated or frozen.

Toasted Sesame Seeds

sesame seeds

1. Heat dry skillet. Add sesame seeds.
2. Stir until light brown, about 2 to 3 minutes, or roast in 300-degree oven
20 minutes.

Szechwan Pepper Oil   SZECHWAN

1 cup vegetable oil
¼ cup red chili peppers, coarsely ground (approximately 1 ounce)

1. Heat oil in wok until moderately hot. Add chili peppers. Cook 3 to 5
minutes on low heat or until oil becomes red.
2. Cool. Store in covered jar indefinitely in refrigerator.

NOTE: Use as seasoning or dip.

Dumpling Sauce

1 tablespoon ginger, chopped fine
1 clove garlic, chopped fine
3 tablespoons light soy sauce
1 tablespoon red wine vinegar

1 teaspoon sugar
¼ teaspoon salt
1 teaspoon pepper oil
  (See Index)

Combine all ingredients. Mix well.

NOTE: Serve as sauce with dumplings.

May be refrigerated. Do not freeze.

Sesame-flavored Dip

½ teaspoon sugar
2 tablespoons sesame seed oil
4 tablespoons light soy sauce

Combine all ingredients. Mix well.

NOTE: Serve with cold meat or vegetables.

May be refrigerated. Do not freeze.

Sesame Seed Paste Sauce

2 tablespoons sesame seed paste, or
   2 tablespoons peanut butter
   diluted in 2 tablespoons water
½ teaspoon salt
2 teaspoons sugar

2 tablespoons light soy sauce
1 tablespoon red wine vinegar
2 tablespoons sesame seed oil
1 teaspoon pepper oil
   (See Index)

Mix ingredients into a smooth, thin sauce.

NOTE: Serve with cooked meat or blanched vegetables (excellent with Mongolian Hot Pot).

May be refrigerated. Do not freeze.

Vegetable Dip

2 tablespoons light soy sauce
1 tablespoon sesame seed oil
1 teaspoon pepper oil
   (See Index)

1 teaspoon sugar
1 tablespoon red wine vinegar

Combine all ingredients. Mix well.

NOTE: Serve with raw vegetables.

May be refrigerated. Do not freeze.

Fruity Fruity Sauce

12 ounces apricot preserves
12 ounces orange marmalade
8 ounces applesauce
8-ounce can of pineapple chunks

1 can Koon Chun Plum Sauce
2 tablespoons white vinegar
2 tablespoons minced ginger

Combine all ingredients in blender and blend until well mixed.

NOTE: Use as a dip.

May be refrigerated. May be frozen.

15

Menu Suggestions

Buffet

In making up a buffet menu, there are three principles to keep in mind: the color scheme, a minimum of last-minute cooking, and what I like to call the balance between land, sea, and air.

As all Chinese dishes are served simultaneously, they should be colorful so as to make the table attractive. Rice is always included on the buffet table. Any fresh fruit will be an excellent dessert.

For the buffet, most of the dishes can be prepared ahead of time. Some of them might require last-minute cooking. The less such effort, the greater the enjoyment for both guests and hosts.

The land, air, and sea parity needs an explanation. Pork, beef, and lamb form the Land Force; the fowls make up the Air Force; all the seafood belongs to the Navy.

If a dish is selected from each group, the meal will be ideally balanced. I once attended a buffet dinner and as the guests were going toward the table, a friend whispered to me, "Your Air Force"! On the table was a preponderance of chicken, duck, and squab.

The following are sample buffet menus that will serve 6.

1. Sour and Peppery Fish Chowder
Chicken Steamed with Chinese
    Sausage
Beef with Onions
Curried Shrimp
Pea Pods with Fresh Mushrooms

2. Meatball Soup
Lychee Chicken with Sweet Sour
    Sauce
Imperial Shrimp
Beef with Asparagus
Chinese Green with Mushrooms
Egg Rolls

3. Hot and Sour Soup
Kung Pao Chicken
Beef with Vermicelli
Crab Meat with Celery Cabbage
Mushrooms and Bamboo Shoots
    (Fried Two Winters)
Won Tons with Sweet Sour Sauce

4. Three-Flavored Sizzling Rice
    Soup
Chicken Wings with Oyster Sauce
Smoked Pomfeit
Beef with Bean Sprouts
Celery Cabbage with Chestnuts

5. Egg Dumpling Soup
Lobster Cantonese
Spinach with Vermicelli
Braised Beef with Turnips
Egg Fu Yung
Fried Spareribs

6. Crab Meat and Asparagus Soup
Jade Chicken
Beef with Crullers
Stuffed Peppers with Shrimp
Six-Minute Broccoli

The Formal Dinner

If you wish a more elaborate meal, here are two menus for a formal dinner party of six. The dishes are served one at a time and rice is usually served just before the dessert or sweet dish. Often noodles take the place of rice at a formal dinner. As a rule the Chinese do not serve egg rolls, won tons, or spareribs at a formal dinner; however, these are very appealing to Westerners.

Hors d' oeuvres:

**Stuffed Mushrooms with Oyster
    Sauce**
Shao Mai

Hors d' oeuvres:

**Chicken Sticks with Sweet Sour
    Sauce**
Shrimp Toast

Entrée:

Chicken Salad with Rice Sticks
Chicken with Walnuts
Beef with Snow Peas
Embroidered Fish Balls
Ants Creeping on the Trees
Shrimp Fried Rice

Entrée:

Jade Soup
"Mama's" Beef
Lemon Chicken
Fish Szechwan Style
Mushrooms with String Beans
Pork Fried Rice

Dessert:

Steamed Apples

Dessert:

Preserved Kumquats

The Banquet

The banquet is the most formal dinner, customarily seating ten to twelve. You will be overwhelmed by the menu. It consists of four cold plates or a large platter containing six to eight varieties of cold dishes. It always includes a hot soup that may be served at the beginning, the middle, or the end of the banquet. The third course consists of hot dishes. Usually four of these are served. The entrée or main course contains four to six dishes. Wine is served throughout the meal. The banquet climaxes with a sweet or fruit for dessert.

Here is an example of a banquet menu to serve 10.

Cold Plate:

Drunken Chicken
Shrimp in Shell, Shanghai Style
Smoked Fish
Mushrooms with Oyster Sauce
Cold Asparagus Salad
Spicy Sweet Sour Cabbage

Soup:

Three Shreds Shark's Fin Soup

Hot Dishes:

Chicken with Pine Nuts
Three-Flavored Scallops
Shrimp with Peas
Mongolian Beef

Entrée:

Peking Duck, or Crispy Duck
Lion's Head
Buddha's Delight
Sweet Sour Fish
Sun Ya Fried Rice

Dessert:

Eight Precious Pudding

16

Pantry Shelf and Storing Information

Many of these items are available in your supermarket and food specialty shops. Some are sold in Oriental stores only. If you have never shopped in an Oriental market, you are in for quite an adventure.

You will see strange and unusual foods, condiments and beautiful vegetables—crisp broccoli, bean sprouts, snow peas (pea pods), the famous long green beans, banana eggplant, bok choy (chinese green), Chinese cabbage, parsley (celantro), and winter melons. Fresh chestnuts are available almost all year. Ginger and garlic are usually sold from bushel baskets. Always be sure the vegetables are fresh when you buy them. They can be refrigerated for a few days, but they taste best when they are cooked the same day they are purchased.

An Oriental store carries seemingly endless varieties of tea, preserves, canned goods, and cookies. If you are lucky enough to find a Chinese meat market, you can buy succulent fresh-roasted ribs, all cuts of pork and, best of all, duck that has been steamed with all fat removed, hanging from the rafters.

You will find the salespeople gracious and happy to help you in Chinese markets. I have translated the pantry items into Chinese. You might want to have this book with you to use as a reference when you shop in Chinatown.

ANISE. A Chinese spice that resembles a star. It imparts a delicate, subtle flavor to meat and poultry. Sold by weight. Store on pantry shelf in tightly covered jar indefinitely.

八角

BAMBOO SHOOTS. Young shoots of tropical bamboo. Sold in cans whole or sliced—best to buy small-sized cans. After opening refrigerate in covered jar of water. Change water twice. Will keep about one week.

筍

BARBECUED ROAST PORK. Almost red in color. Sold by the pound in Chinese delicatessens and meat shops. Will keep in refrigerator about five days. Can be frozen.

叉燒

BEAN CURD. 1. Fresh bean curd: Made of pureed soybeans, then formed into cakes 1-inch thick and 4-inches square. When cooked, it absorbs the flavor of other ingredients. It is sold in plastic containers in the refrigerated section. It is also called To-fu. Will keep in its own container in refrigerator about one week.

鮮豆腐

五香豆腐干

2. Brown bean curd: Dried pressed bean curd, well-flavored. Sold in plastic bags in the refrigerated section. Will keep in refrigerator about one week. Can be frozen.

3. Dried bean curd sheets: Dried, paper-thin sheets. Sold in packages of 8 ounces and up. Store on pantry shelf for a few months.

豆腐衣

4. White pressed bean curd: Sold in plastic wrap in refrigerated section. Will keep in refrigerator about one week. Can be frozen.

白豆腐干

5. Soybean pudding: A very soft, fine bean curd in water. Sold in refrigerated section. Will keep in refrigerator about one week. Do not freeze.

豆腐花

BEAN SAUCE. Also known as brown bean sauce or brown bean paste. Made of soybeans, flour, salt, and water. It is salty and pungent. Sold in cans. After opening refrigerate in a tightly covered jar. Will keep indefinitely.

原晒鼓

BIRDS' NESTS. Sold in 1-pound boxes. Store on pantry shelf for a few months.

燕窩

BLACK BEANS (fermented). Salty black beans. Used for seasoning. Sold in plastic bags of 4 ounces and up. Store on pantry shelf in tightly covered jar indefinitely.

豆鼓

BROWN RICE MEAL. Used as a seasoning. Sold by weight. Store on pantry shelf in tightly covered jar indefinitely.

炒米粉

CELLOPHANE NOODLES. Also known as bean thread or vermicelli. Made from mung bean flour. When used in soup, must be pre-soaked. Not necessary to soak when deep frying. They will pop up immediately. Sold in plastic bags of two ounces and up. Store on pantry shelf indefinitely.

粉絲

CHESTNUTS (dried). Available in Chinese markets. Soak overnight before using. Sold in plastic bags. Store on pantry shelf in tightly covered jar indefinitely.

栗子

CHICKEN STOCK. See Chapter 1 for Helpful Hints. Also see Index for Basic Chicken Stock recipe.

CHILI PASTE WITH GARLIC. Made with hot pepper and garlic. Used mostly in Szechwan dishes. Sold in 8-ounce bottles. Refrigerate after opening. Will keep indefinitely.

四川辣椒醬

CHILI SAUCE.   Made with chili, onions, lemons, sweet potatoes, and
辣　　　　vinegar. Adds spice to dishes. Sold in bottles. After opening
椒　　　　refrigerate. Will keep indefinitely.
醬

CLOUD EARS. Also known as tree ears or fungus. Must be soaked in hot
　　　　　water before using. Cook with vegetables, chicken, meat, and
木　　　　soul. Sold in plastic bags of 2 ounces and up. Store on
耳　　　　pantry shelf in tightly covered jar indefinitely.

CRAB APPLE WAFER. Also known as plum wafer. Made of crab apples
山　　　　and sugar. Sold in cylindrical packages. Store on pantry
楂　　　　shelf indefinitely.
片

CURRY PASTE AND CURRY POWDER. The brands that are made in
茄　　　　India are the best. Sold in bottles. Store on pantry shelf
厘　　　　indefinitely.
粉醬

DATES (Chinese). Red in color, dried, the size of marbles. Sold in 4- to
　　　　　8-ounce plastic bags. Store on pantry shelf in tightly covered
紅　　　　jar for a few months.
棗

DRIED ORANGE PEEL. A dried spice made from orange rinds. Used
　　　　　for flavoring meat and poultry. Sold in plastic bags. Store on
陳　　　　pantry shelf in tightly covered jar indefinitely.
皮

DRIED SOYBEANS. Yellow in color. Used in many dishes. Sold in 1-
　　　　　pound plastic bags. Store on pantry shelf in tightly covered
黃　　　　jar indefinitely.
豆

EGG ROLL WRAPPINGS. Dough in which to place the filling of the egg
　　　　　roll. There are two kinds. The Cantonese are square. The
春　　　　Shanghai are thinner and round. (I prefer the latter.)
卷　　　　Usually sold in 2-pound packages. Will keep in refrigerator
皮　　　　about five days. Can be frozen.

FENNEL SEEDS. A dried spice used for flavoring meat and poultry. Sold in plastic bags. Store on pantry shelf in tightly covered jar indefinitely.

茴
香

FIVE-SPICE POWDER. Combination of five spices. Used for flavoring. Sold in plastic bags. Store on pantry shelf in tightly covered jar for about six months.

五
香
粉

GINGER ROOT. Fresh. Very important seasoning in Chinese cooking. There is no substitute for it. Sold by piece or by weight. Peel and put in jar with sherry; cover tightly. Will keep in refrigerator indefinitely.

薑

GINKGO NUTS. Have hard white shells. Sold in 10-ounce cans. After opening refrigerate in covered jar of water. Change water twice. Will keep about one week. Can be frozen.

白
果

GOLDEN LILIES. Dried and pale in color. Also known as golden needles or tiger lilies. Add flavor to meat, fish, poultry, and soup. Sold in plastic bags. Store on pantry shelf in tightly covered jar indefinitely.

金
針

HAIR SEAWEED. Very fine, resembles hair. Used with vegetable dishes. Sold in plastic bags. Store on pantry shelf in tightly covered jar indefinitely.

髮
菜

HAM (Virginia, Smithfield). The nearest tasting to Chinese ham. Very salty. Sold by weight. Wrap in plastic. Will keep in refrigerator for many months. Can be frozen.

火
腿

HOISIN SAUCE. Spicy sauce used in many dishes. Sold in 1-pound cans.
海鮮醬   After opening refrigerate in tightly covered jar. Will keep
indefinitely.

HOT PEPPER OIL. Spicy homemade oil used a great deal for seasoning
辣油   Szechwan dishes. Sold in bottles. Will keep in refrigerator
for a few months.

LONG-GRAIN RICE FLOUR. A ground flour made from long-grain rice.
粘米粉   Used for making turnip cake and snacks. Sold in 1-pound
packages. Store on pantry shelf for a few months.

LOTUS SEEDS. Dried white seeds. Must be cooked. Sold in plastic bags.
蓮心   Store on pantry shelf in tightly covered jar indefinitely.

LYCHEE. A tropical fruit. Delicious in sweet sour sauce. Sold in cans in
荔枝   heavy syrup. Refrigerate in a tightly covered jar. Will keep
several days.

MUSHROOMS (Chinese). Dried and black—must be soaked in boiling
冬菇   water before using. Used in many dishes. Sold in plastic
bags. Store on pantry shelf in tightly covered jar indefinitely.

MUSTARD (Chinese). Used for dipping when diluted with water. Sold in
芥末粉   powdered form. Store on pantry shelf in tightly covered jar
indefinitely.

OILS. See chapter 1 for use of oil in cooking.

OYSTER SAUCE. Thick, flavored sauce made from oyster extract. Adds
蠔油   flavor to meat and poultry. Sold in bottles of 8 ounces and
up. Store on pantry shelf for a few months.

PEPPERCORNS. Used to make peppercorn salt and for seasoning. (See Index for recipe.) Sold in plastic bags. Store on pantry shelf in tightly covered jar indefinitely.

四
川
花
椒

PICKLED PLUMS. Preserved plums. Used for seasoning meat and poultry. Sold in jars. After opening refrigerate in tightly covered jar. Will keep a few months.

酸
梅

PICKLED SNOW CABBAGE. Preserved salted cabbage. Delicious with pork. Sold in cans. After opening refrigerate in tightly covered jar. Will keep a few months.

雪
裡
紅

PLUM SAUCE. Used as a condiment. Sold in jars or cans. After opening refrigerate in tightly covered jar. Will keep a few months.

酸
梅
醬

PRESERVED CUCUMBER. Used in cooking many dishes. Sold in cans. After opening refrigerate in tightly covered jar. Will keep indefinitely.

醬
黃
瓜

PRESERVED GINGER. Used in sweet and sour dishes for color and flavoring. Delicious as a garnish for chicken salads. Sold in jars. After opening refrigerate in tightly covered jar. Will keep indefinitely.

紅
薑

PRESERVED MIXED VEGETABLES. Used for seasoning, especially in sweet and sour dishes. Mixture of different kinds of sweet vegetables. Sold in cans. After opening refrigerate in tightly covered jar. Will keep indefinitely.

雜
錦
菜
絲

PRESERVED SZECHWAN VEGETABLE. Used for seasoning. Sold in cans. After opening refrigerate in tightly covered jar. Will keep indefinitely.

四
川
搾
菜

PRESERVED YUNNAN CABBAGE. Flavors meat. Sold in 1-pound plastic bags. After opening refrigerate in tightly covered jar. Will keep indefinitely.

RED BEANS. Used in pastries and sweet foods. Sold in 1-pound plastic bags. Store on pantry shelf indefinitely.

RED PEPPER. Dried. Whole, crushed, or ground. Used for seasoning. Sold in plastic bags. Store on pantry shelf indefinitely.

RED WINE VINEGAR. Used for cooking and as a dip. Sold in bottles. Store on pantry shelf indefinitely.

RICE (Glutinous). Also known as sweet rice. Used for making dumplings, sweet dishes, and poultry stuffing. Store on pantry shelf indefinitely.

RICE (Red). Dyed raw rice for coloring food. Sold loose by the ounce. Store on pantry shelf indefinitely.

RICE (White Long-Grain). Sold in 5- and 10-pound bags in Chinatown. (Supermarkets sell it in small plastic bags.) Store on pantry shelf indefinitely.

RICE NOODLE (Chow Fun). Used combined with meats and poultry. Sold in plastic bags in 1-pound packages in refrigerated section. Will keep in refrigerator for three days. Can be frozen.

RICE FLOUR. Ground from rice. Used in sweet dishes and snacks. Store on pantry shelf indefinitely.

RICE FLOUR (Sweet). Made from glutinous rice. Used for making dumplings and sweet dishes. Store on pantry shelf for a few months.

糯
米
粉

RICE STICKS. Dried (Py Mai Fun) Used in soups and many other dishes. Sold in ½-pound packages and up. Store on pantry shelf indefinitely.

排
米
粉

SATE PASTE. Used for flavoring meat. Sold in bottles and cans. After opening refrigerate. Will keep a few months.

沙
茶
醬

SAUSAGE (Chinese). Made with liver and pork. Sold in plastic bags in 1-pound packages. Rewrap in plastic. Refrigerate for one month. May be frozen.

香
腸

SESAME PASTE (OR SESAME SEED PASTE). Peanut butter can be substituted. Used as seasoning. Sold in jars. Will keep a few months in refrigerator.

芝
蔴
醬

SESAME SEEDS. Sold in plastic bags of 4 ounces and up. Store on pantry shelf indefinitely.

芝
蔴

SESAME SEED OIL. See chapter 1 for use of oils in Chinese cooking. Will keep indefinitely in refrigerator.

蔴
油

SHARK'S FIN. Dried. Must soak before using. Sold in ½- to 1-pound boxes. Store on pantry shelf indefinitely.

魚
翅

SHRIMP (Chinese Dried). Have a sharp flavor. Used in small amounts in cooking. Store on pantry shelf in tightly covered jar for many months.

蝦
米

SOY SAUCE (Light and Dark). One of the most important seasonings in 生老 抽抽 Chinese cooking. Sold in bottles from 12 ounces up. Store on pantry shelf indefinitely.

STRAW MUSHROOMS. Delicious with crab meat. Sold in cans. After 草菇 opening refrigerate in covered jar of water. Change water twice. Will keep several weeks.

TEA. See chapter 13. Store on pantry shelf indefinitely. 茶葉

VERMICELLI. See Cellophane Noodles.

WATER CHESTNUTS. Used as a vegetable with meats and poultry. 馬蹄 Delicious with snow peas. Sold in cans. After opening refrigerate in covered jar of water. Change water twice a week. Will keep several weeks.

WATER NOODLES (Chinese Fresh). Noodles made with flour and 生麵 water. Delicious in soup and stir-fried dishes. Will keep about five days in refrigerator. Can be frozen.

WINE. Used as a seasoning in many dishes. Rice wine can be used. (See 酒 Index for recipe.) Dry sherry is used most frequently. Store sherry on pantry shelf indefinitely. Rice wine must be refrigerated in a tightly covered jar. Will keep for many months.

WINE BALL. The "pill" with which to make Chinese rice wine. Store on 酒藥 pantry shelf in tightly covered jar. Will keep indefinitely.

WON TON WRAPPINGS. Dough in which to place won ton and shao 餛飩皮 mai fillings. Made round and square. Sold in 1-pound packages. Will keep in refrigerator about one week. Can be frozen.

17

Chinese Markets

Should you not have an Oriental food shop in your city, the following is a list that will assist you and facilitate your shopping. Asterisk(*) denotes that mail orders may be placed.

Arizona

Phoenix Produce Company
202 South 3rd Street
Phoenix, 85004

Tang's Market
4102 North 24th Street
Phoenix, 85016

California

B & C Market*
711 North Broadway
Los Angeles, 90012

Kwong on Lung Importers*
680 North Spring Street
Los Angeles, 90012

Yee Sing Chong Company
966 North Hill Street
Los Angeles, 90012

Oakland Market
378 8th Street
Oakland, 94607

Wo Soon Product Company*
1210 Stockton Street
San Francisco, 94133

Illinois

Dong Kee Co.*
2252 South Wentworth Avenue
Chicago, 60616

Oriental Food Market
7411 North Clark Street
Chicago, 60626

Massachusetts

Chong Lung
18 Hudson
Boston, 02111

Wing Wing Imported Groceries
79 Harrison Avenue
Boston, 02111

Michigan

Seoul Oriental Market*
23031 Beach Road
Southfield 48075

Chinese Asia Trading Company*
734 S. Washington Road
Royal Oak 48067

China Merchandise Corporation*
31642 John Road
Madison Heights 48071

New York

Yuit Hing Market Corporation*
23 Pell Street
New York, 10013

Wing Fat Company*
35 Mott Street
New York 10013
(mail order minimum is $15.00)

Ohio

Soya Food Products*
2356 Wyoming Avenue
Cincinnati, 45214

Washington, D.C.

Mee Wah Lung Company*
608 H Street, N.W.
Washington, 20001

Texas

Oriental Import-Export Company*
2009 Polk Street
Houston, 77003

Washington

Uwajimaya, Inc.*
519 Sixth Avenue South
Seattle, 98104

Wah Yong Co.*
416 Eighth Avenue South
Seattle, 98104

Canada

Wing Noodles Ltd.
1009, rue Côté
Montreal, P.Q.
Canada H2Z 1L1

Wing Tong Trading Co.
137 Dundas St. W.
Toronto, Ontario
Canada M5G 1Z3

Index